The Behavior
of Women and Men

LAWRENCE S. WRIGHTSMAN
Consulting Editor

The Behavior of Women and Men
Kay Deaux, Purdue University

**Research Projects in Social Psychology:
An Introduction to Methods**
Michael King, California State University, Chico
Michael Ziegler, York University

**Three Views of Man: Perspectives from Sigmund Freud,
B. F. Skinner, and Carl Rogers**
Robert D. Nye, State University of New York, College at New Paltz

Theories of Personality
Duane Schultz, American University

Interpersonal Behavior
Harry C. Triandis, University of Illinois at Urbana-Champaign

The Behavior of Women and Men

Kay Deaux

Purdue University

Brooks/Cole Publishing Company
Monterey, California

A Division of Wadsworth Publishing Company, Inc.

Consulting Editor: Lawrence S. Wrightsman

ISBN: 0-8185-0177-4
L.C. Catalog Card No.: 75-23856
Printed in the United States of America

10 9 8 7 6 5 4

Acquisition Editor: *William H. Hicks*
Manuscript Editor: *Joan Marsh*
Production Editor: *Konrad Kerst*
Interior & Cover Design: *John Edeen*
Photographs: *Catherine DeLattre*
Typesetting: *Instant Type, Monterey, California*

Preface

Few people would claim ignorance on the subject of women and men. Yet despite the general interest, many readers may not be aware of the extensive body of research that exists on this topic—research that in many instances counters the simple generalizations that we all form about how adult men and women typically behave.

This book is my attempt to bring together a considerable amount of information about the behavior of women and men. By presenting a new integration of research in the area, yet describing these findings in a readable way, I hope the book will appeal to those who have never taken a psychology course as well as to those advanced students and investigators who want a convenient annotated summary of the current research on sex differences and similarities.

My intent is to present not a "psychology of women" but a discussion of women *and* men and of the advantages and disadvantages of both sex roles. However, the book is quite appropriate for courses in the psychology of women and women's studies programs. My own guess is that in the next few years we will see more courses dealing with sex differences and sex roles of both women and men, as opposed to the one-sided "psychology of women" or "psychology of men" point of view, and for this audience the book should be well-suited. In addition, I feel that the writing style and length of the book make it useful as a supplement in general social psychology or introductory psychology courses.

My own interest in the topic of the sexes developed gradually. My training as a social psychologist was very traditional, and for several years after graduate school I diligently pursued topics such as attitude change and interpersonal attraction that were, and continue to be, in the mainstream of social-psychological research. Yet as questions about women and men became a major issue in the society outside of my laboratory, my mainstream focus was diverted. It occurred to me that as a social psychologist I might add something to the issues that were being debated. Certainly the theories of attitude change, stereotyping, attribution, and attraction must have something to say about the behavior of the sexes. In my research, I began to pursue these connections. I soon discovered two facts of life. First, at that time such a pursuit was not wholly acceptable to some more traditional social psychologists. Success, I was told, would come with mainstream pursuits. Yet a second discovery diminished the impact of the first. Social psychologists had indeed discovered a great deal about the behavior of men and women. Although these differences were generally relegated to a footnote or minor paragraph in the overall report, the quantity of the findings was impressive. Someone, it occurred to me, should attempt to integrate these multiple findings to find out what we do know about the behavior of women and men in social situations. I decided to be that someone, and this book represents the results of those efforts.

Many of the topics that are currently "hot" in discussions about women and men are included: for example, the stereotypes our society holds, the issue of fear of success in women (and men), and androgyny as an alternative to masculinity or femininity. In addition, many other areas of social behavior are considered: altruism, aggression, nonverbal and verbal behavior, self-esteem and self-evaluation, cooperation, competition, interpersonal attraction, and the behavior of women and men in groups. In each case, the relevant literature is covered and an attempt is made to summarize just what the differences and similarities between women and men are. Particular attention is also given to the influence of situations and environments, for it turns out that the behavior of women and men varies considerably from situation to situation. Only by considering both the sex and the situation can we arrive at a real appreciation of the complexity of women and men and human behavior.

I could not have written this book without the help of a great many people. Those who provided helpful comments on one or more chapters include: Elizabeth Rice Allgeier, Paul Bell, Richard Borden, Diane Boss, Len Bickman, Donn Byrne, James Dabbs, Jr., Jeffrey Fisher, Alan Gross, Mary Harris, Richard Heslin, Jerald Jellison, Arnie Kahn, Kathleen Kelley, Cheris Kramer, Gerald Leventhal, Lawrence Messé, Arie Nadler, Michelle Nguyen, Marvin Rytting, Janet Spence, and Janet Taynor. The entire manuscript was read by Francine Gordon of Stanford University, Michele Hoffnung of Quinnipiac College, Joy Stapp of the University of California, Berkeley, Dalmas Taylor of the University of Maryland, Leonore Tiefer of Colorado State University, and Michele Wittig of California State University, Northridge; each of these persons offered valuable suggestions that contributed to the final product. Frances Cherry and Elizabeth Farris not only provided comments on nearly every chapter but have both been a part of many conversations that contributed to the ideas developed in this book. Janice Pollister was a marvelous typist, undangling my participles and offering much-needed encouragement along the way. The photographs in the book are the work of Catherine DeLattre, who made a difficult job enjoyable.

My support from Brooks/Cole was terribly important. Consulting editor Lawrence Wrightsman provided advice and encouragement throughout the project, and Bill Hicks and his staff were a pleasure to work with. Finally, I must be thankful at a more personal level to Jim O'Connor, who has furnished insight and excitement to my work and my life and has proved Nietzsche wrong.

Kay Deaux

Contents

The Behavior
of Women and Men

Chapter 1

Perspectives
on Women and Men

There are many ways to look at the people of the world. We can consider the style of the Italians, the habits of Nigerians, or the customs of the citizens of Borneo. Writers have talked about differences between blacks and whites, or between the young and the old, or between rich and poor. Still other observers have categorized people by height, or weight, or color of eyes. Yet perhaps the most basic division of all is that between men and women. From the garden of Eden to the present day, people have debated the similarities and differences between women and men.

While interest in the topic has never waned, the debate has accelerated in recent years. Political movements for women's equality have revived and expanded the goals of the earlier suffrage movement of the 1920s. Television shows have been devoted to an exploration of the sexes. Men and women alike are joining discussion groups, having consciousness-raising sessions, and finding other formats to consider the nature of sex roles. In fact, it becomes increasingly rare to pick up a magazine, read the evening newspaper, or engage in casual conversation without encountering some discussion of the behavior of men and women.

Scientists have not been oblivious to these concerns. On the contrary, hundreds of investigations have attempted to establish what differences exist between the sexes and to isolate the causes of these differences. Early research tended to construct catalogs of sex differences, generally focusing on abilities and personality traits. With a flurry of measurement, a lengthy list of differences between men and women was compiled. Armed with evidence of such differences, other investigators sought causes. Some looked to biological and hereditary factors, while others concentrated on the socialization process and the interaction between parent and child. Still others traveled to distant societies, attempting to determine the generality of male and female behavior. Yet while the search for causes has continued, two eminent investigators have recently argued that very few of the differences that were previously thought to exist have actually been supported by the experimental research.[1]*

*All footnotes appear numerically at the end of the book.

THE DEVELOPMENT OF A
SOCIAL-PSYCHOLOGICAL PERSPECTIVE

In the face of such apparent confusion, you might wonder why another investigator would enter the fray. I do so because I think another view can be offered on the persisting question of sex differences. This view originates from my own field of social psychology, a field that I believe has a unique contribution to make toward understanding the behavior of women and men.

As a social psychologist, I have been trained to look at the impact of situational factors. How can variations in the environment lead to differences in observed behavior? Traditionally, social psychology has been concerned with this general question as it is applied to social behaviors such as altruism, aggression, cooperation, competition, and interpersonal attraction. Individual differences in such behaviors have been of less concern. Sex differences in particular have frequently been considered a nuisance variable, and often social psychologists have limited their investigations to one sex only in order to avoid the discovery that men and women act differently.[2] Yet in spite of this benign neglect, social psychology has discovered a great deal about the ways in which men and women behave. In nearly every area of social behavior, differences between women and men have been observed.

Unlike earlier perspectives, however, a social-psychological approach will not lead us to conclude that men always act one way and women always act another. Instead, this perspective will require us to look at both the person (specifically, the sex of the person) and the situation. Our conclusions will be phrased in terms of interactions between these two factors.

To make this viewpoint clearer, let's consider an example. Suppose that you are interested in the responses of men and women to humorous cartoons. You select 10 cartoons and record the giggles. Your results show that men laugh harder than women do at five of the cartoons, while women chuckle more heartily at the remaining five. What would you conclude? The simplest answer would be that men and women do not differ in their humor quotients. Both sexes laugh equally often. Many people concerned with sex differences have used just this approach, summing up studies and seeing which sex shows a particular behavior more often. When the numbers for the sexes are even, a conclusion of no difference follows.

Now let's consider a social-psychological approach to this same question of humor. Concerned with situations, our social psychologist looks more carefully at the kinds of cartoons used. This inquiry reveals that five of the cartoons were taken from *Playboy* magazine, while the other five came from *Playgirl.* Sensing a possible pattern, our social psychologist looks back to the responses of men and women and finds that women were laughing at *Playgirl* cartoons while men preferred the jokes of *Playboy.* "No difference" now seems to be an overly simplified conclusion. If both the person and the situation are considered, we can make more specific statements about the humor appreciation of women and men.

Such a perspective is certainly more complex than some of the earlier views. Yet the evidence seems to require such complexity. Men are not always more altruistic than women, and women are not always more cooperative than men. However, in most instances, we can find patterns in the apparent randomness, and these patterns will advance our understanding of the behavior of women and men.

One word of caution is in order. In taking a social-psychological perspective, or in adopting any other view toward differences between men and women, we are talking about *averages.* For example, men on the average are taller than women. Yet there are some very tall women and some very short men living in the world today. In intellectual abilities, personality traits, and social behaviors, the same broad distribution of characteristics is found. We have not split the world into two separate parts when we discuss the nature of men and women. Rather we are simply focusing on two trends that often point in different directions. This concept of overlap should be remembered throughout the discussion that follows.

The social-psychological perspective of this book, while unique, has not developed in a vacuum. Before reviewing the specific aims of the book, let's briefly consider the contributions of earlier approaches.

THE CATALOG PERSPECTIVE

Hundreds of studies have reported similarities and differences between men and women. Frequently, these findings have been almost accidental: for example, in developing a new personality scale, an investigator may discover that men and women score differently. On other occasions, the specific concern has been whether men and women are different in aggressiveness, in moral development, or in intellectual abilities. I would guess that a sex difference has been reported at one time or another for virtually every human characteristic known to scientists. A number of catalogs of these differences exist.[3]

Looking historically at the research on sex differences, however, we find that conclusions of differences between men and women have frequently been in error. Too often, an investigator has concluded that there are basic differences when only one or two studies exist. A notable exception to this pattern is the recent work of Eleanor Maccoby and Carol Jacklin.[4] After a careful analysis of all the available evidence, these two investigators conclude that very few differences between women and men have been supported. Many "mythical" sex differences do not stand up under the scrutiny of these two careful analysts.

Are there any established differences between the sexes? Maccoby and Jacklin find solid evidence for only four behaviors. Women are superior to men on tests of verbal ability, while men excel on tests of mathematical ability. In both instances, these differences are not observed during early childhood but show divergence only after adolescence. In addition, the authors conclude that men and boys are consistently more aggressive than women and girls. A fourth difference is found in visual-spatial ability. Adolescent boys and men perform better on tasks that require the isolation of one particular shape in a complex pattern of shapes.

These authors do not conclude that no other differences between men and women can exist. In fact, they suggest a number of areas, such as anxiety, compliance, competitiveness, and dominance, in which it is unsafe to draw any conclusions. Differences may exist, but the research has been inadequate to test the questions.

In the course of this book, we will have cause to re-examine a number of these areas. While not refuting a conclusion of no overall differences, we will see consistent patterns within the total picture.

THE BIOLOGICAL PERSPECTIVE

No one doubts that there are some biological differences between men and women. Beyond acknowledging the obvious physical and reproductive differences, however, investigators have attempted to determine how the behavior of men and women may be influenced by biological, physiological, and hormonal factors.

In some instances, this search for biological roots has relied on a faulty assessment of the differences between men and women. For example, one group of investigators has proposed a complex model that relates sex differences in the activity of the central nervous system to sex differences in intellectual abilities.[5] Unfortunately for this model, the recent analyses of intellectual abilities in men and women do not show these assumed differences and hence cause problems for the entire explanatory chain.[6]

Other research done from a biological perspective has focused on the effects of hormones on behavior, generally using rats and monkeys. The most frequent procedure has been to inject young animals with sex-related hormones and to observe the adult behavior of these same animals. Evidence from these animal studies suggests that sex-related hormones do act on the brain during early critical periods of development and in turn influence such behaviors as aggression in the adult animal.[7]

Other evidence also points to a biological basis for aggression.[8] While the hormone balance of humans is not a reasonable area for experimental manipulation, other sources of information can be tapped. First of all, differences between males and females in aggression levels appear early in life, before socialization is assumed to have much impact. Second, men have shown more aggression than women in nearly every society studied. The fact that these observations are consistent with the results of hormone studies leads to some confidence in the belief that aggression is in part biologically influenced.

The difference between men and women in visual-spatial ability also appears to have a genetic component.[9] Results from genetic studies point to the influence of a recessive sex-linked gene, which occurs among men more often than women. (Don't conclude that this gene never occurs among women or that it is always found among men. There is simply a difference in the frequency of occurrence). Few other characteristics of women and men have any strong degree of biological support.

Given the consistent difference in aggression and spatial ability between women and men and their apparent biological base, you might wonder whether social factors play any part in these behaviors. Two important points should be made regarding the effect of biological factors on behavior in general and sex differences in particular. First, the inherited component, when it exists, represents only a tendency or a readiness to behave in a certain way. In the case of aggression, for example, a person must learn *how* to be aggressive and *when* to be aggressive through experience. Men may have a head start on this process, but they are not born with all of the necessary equipment. A second and related point is that experience can modify the inherited component. Heredity does not mean inflexibility, and, contrary to Freud, biology is not necessarily destiny. Through experience, a girl can develop a full repertoire of aggressive behaviors, and, through other training, a boy may develop into a very passive creature. Heredity may provide the raw materials, but experience can drastically alter their form.

THE SOCIALIZATION PERSPECTIVE

This experience has been a concern for developmental psychologists. As either an alternative or a supplement to hereditary explanations of sex differences, the socialization explanation relies on particular experiences the young child has in the course of growing up.

A major focus has been on the ways in which parents interact with children. Do parents encourage some behaviors in one sex while discouraging the same behaviors in the other sex? Early studies suggested that there were a great many differences in the treatment of boys and girls. It has been widely assumed, for example, that parents are more tolerant of aggression in boys and encourage more dependency in girls. However, Maccoby and Jacklin have again forced a reconsideration of these assumptions.[10] Carefully analyzing the research on parent-child interactions, these investigators find no difference in parents' tolerance for either of these behaviors. Parents (at least mothers, who have been studied the most) discourage aggressive behavior in both boys and girls and show no difference in their response to dependency as a function of the child's sex.

While the majority of studies show no difference in the socialization of boys and girls, there are some exceptions. For example, parents treat infants somewhat differently. Young boys are given more physical stimulation, while there is a tendency for girls to receive more vocal stimulation. As children grow older, other differences in the reactions of parents emerge. Parents use physical punishment much more often with boys, yet at the same time they are more likely to praise boys when they do something well.[11]

Differences are more apparent when it comes to specifically sex-related activities. Parents agree that they have certain expectations for their children: boys should not be feminine and girls should not be masculine. To encourage the appropriate development, parents buy such toys as trucks and sports equipment for boys, while they give dolls and cooking sets to girls. Furthermore, the evidence again suggests that these socialization pressures are stronger for boys than for girls: the girl who is a "tomboy" is discouraged less than the boy who is a "sissy."

While the direct pressure of parents is an important part of socialization, other factors can influence the child's learning as well. Psychologist Walter Mischel has argued persuasively for the importance of observational learning and modeling in the child's development of sex-typed behavior.[12] Children can imitate what they see, and once they learn that men and women are different they may begin to model their behaviors after persons of their same sex. This process of learning through observation is not limited to live models. Children also learn what is appropriate for their sex by watching television and reading books. Television programs and commercials often present a highly stereotyped picture of men and women,[13] and children's readers are equally limited in the range of options they present.[14] If the tendency to imitate is strong, then boys and girls may learn very different behaviors from the media.

These socialization experiences are an important basis for developing a view of sex differences that includes both the person and the situation. We need to learn more about specific experiences that affect the development of men and women. While research in this area has established some general patterns, we again need to ask for a finer analysis. For example, most of the research on parent-child interaction has involved only the mother. Perhaps the father plays a critical role in the socialization of children, discriminating more between boys and girls. Or perhaps mothers, while discouraging aggression in both sexes, do so on different occasions. Once again, I think we have to look beyond the generalities to the specific situations. Boys and girls may learn the same behaviors but learn to do them in quite different situations, and these original learning experiences could have a direct link to the patterns that we find in adult women and men.

THE CROSS-CULTURAL PERSPECTIVE

A number of investigators have turned to the study of other societies, attempting to establish patterns in the behavior of men and women that can generalize beyond a single culture. In many cases, these investigations have represented an attempt to learn whether biology or socialization is a more important cause. For example, if a difference between men and women is found consistently across a variety of societies, then we can have more faith in a biological component. Aggression is a case in point. Yet in most other behaviors, there is considerable variation across societies, suggesting that socialization plays an important role.

More interesting evidence from the cross-cultural research concerns the relationship between the particular needs of a society and the behaviors of men and women in that society. These investigations come very close to the present perspective, because they consider how specific situations will lead to specific behaviors. Barry, Bacon, and Child found that societies that put a premium on physical strength tend to make stronger distinctions between the appropriate behavior for men and women.[15] More industrialized societies in which physical strength is less essential show less sex-role differentiation. In another society studied, a shortage of girls led to the use of boys in child-caring duties. Presumably because of their different set of experiences, these boys appeared less aggressive and less dominant than boys in other societies. [16]

In some cases, observers have even been able to document changes in the behavior of women and men that parallel changes in the society's needs. Patricia Draper has recently reported such developments among the !Kung people of Africa. [17] For hundreds of years, these people lived as nomadic hunters and gatherers, and men and women shared the work of the group on an equal basis. Recently, however, many of the !Kung have shifted to a more sedentary village existence. In these new circumstances, a more specific division of labor between men and women has developed, and the young boys and girls are being trained for different tasks. It would be interesting to return to the !Kung people in 20 or 30 years. We would expect that the differences between men and women will be much greater in that society in the future than they are today.

In many respects, the cross-cultural approach to sex differences is a large-scale social-psychology laboratory. Looking across many societies, these investigators have begun to isolate specific conditions that foster particular differences in the behavior of men and women. Our own approach is similar. However, instead of societal patterns, we'll be looking at particular situational factors. The disadvantage of our approach, in contrast to this broader perspective, is that most of the discussion will be based on studies of men and women (and frequently only college men and women) in the United States. Only future research can tell us whether men and women in other societies, or even in subcultures within this country, will behave in exactly the same way. On the other hand, our more limited approach has advantages as well. With more access to the men and women involved and with the ability to specifically alter aspects of the situation that seem to be important, we can establish more precise relationships between the situation and the person. Understanding one society is a starting point and a necessary step toward the ultimate goal of understanding not only the nature of men and women but human behavior in general.

ELEMENTS OF A SOCIAL-PSYCHOLOGICAL PERSPECTIVE

In adopting a social-psychological perspective, we'll constantly be giving consideration to both the person (the average woman or man) and the situation. In using both of these concepts, we'll try to find patterns in the behavior of men and women that are consistent. Even the sex of the person will be considered both as an attribute of the individual and as one aspect of the situation. For example, in some instances we will look at how people react to a man or a woman—how the sex of the other person in a situation can affect behavior. For example, are people in general more helpful toward a man or toward a woman? Is it easier to talk about yourself to a woman or a man? On other occasions (and sometimes on the same occasions) we'll be speaking of sex as a subject variable—of men and women acting the same or differently in a particular situation. Are women more cooperative than men? Do men make more eye contact than women? In addition, we'll be looking at the specific interactions of one sex with the other in all these situations.

We will begin this investigation by considering what people think about men and women. What are the general attitudes and stereotypes that people hold, and how do these stereotypes affect other judgments? These questions are the concerns of Chapters 2 and 3. Having considered the view of an outsider, we'll then move to the view of an insider. What do men and women think about themselves? In Chapter 4, we'll look at the self-evaluation patterns of men and women, and in Chapter 5 we'll consider the achievement-oriented behaviors men and women show. From these intrapersonal topics, we will move on to a survey of the behavior of women and men as they relate to others: in communication (Chapter 6), in altruism (Chapter 7), and in aggression (Chapter 8). Other forms of interaction will be discussed in Chapters 9 and 10, as we deal with cooperation, competition, and group behavior, and in Chapter 11, when we cover specific male-female attraction and interaction. Finally, in Chapter 12, we'll tackle the general question of masculinity and femininity, the new concept of androgyny, and the relationship of these concepts to social behavior.

In the course of this exploration, we will cover a good deal of material that has originated in social-psychology laboratories. Yet the perspective itself is not limited to social psychologists. Our major concern is to develop an understanding of the behavior of men and women as they behave in a variety of situations and circumstances. Other disciplines have already contributed some important guidelines, and the present view is an attempt to enlarge our understanding of ourselves and the women and men around us.

Chapter 2

Stereotypes
of Women and Men:
Personality Traits

*Women are ever in extremes; they are either better
or worse than men.*

La Bruyère

*Women are wiser than men because they know less
and understand more.*

James Stephens

*Men have broad and large chests, and small narrow hips,
and are more understanding than women, who have but
small and narrow chests, and broad hips, to the end they
should remain at home, sit still, keep house, and
bring up the children.*

Martin Luther

*I'm not denyin' the women are foolish:
God Almighty made 'em to match the men.*

George Eliot

What do people think men and women are like? Are there
personality traits that you would consider to be characteristic of
most men? Are there other traits that you think most women have?
In later chapters, we'll consider how men and women actually do
differ from each other. In this chapter and the following one,
however, we'll be concerned with how people *think* men and women
differ.

The quotations at the beginning of this chapter are only a small
sample of the tremendous number of observations that have been
made, throughout the centuries, on the essence of women and men.
Philosophers, politicians, and comedians alike have felt obliged to
comment on the differences between the sexes. Yet while the sources
of these observations show great variety, psychologists have found
that there is substantial agreement in the beliefs that people hold

regarding the nature of men and women. Because these assumptions about the personality traits of men and women are widely shared and are believed to apply to nearly all men and women as members of their respective groups, they can be considered *stereotypes*. Just as people are often willing to infer the characteristics of a teen-ager or a Mexican or an opera singer, they will also draw conclusions about someone who is male or female based on that fact alone.

STEREOTYPES OF MEN AND WOMEN

In an early study of sex stereotypes, Caroline MacBrayer asked a group of college students to complete a series of open-ended questions about the opposite sex.[1] Some examples of the statements she used are "I believe most women ... " and "What I like least about men ...." Students were to finish each sentence in any way they wanted, and MacBrayer coded the responses in terms of their favorability. Her results clearly showed that women were more favorable in their impressions of men than men were in their evaluations of women.

In a similar study, McKee and Sherriffs asked subjects to select traits that they felt pertained to males and those that pertained to females.[2] Once again, differences were apparent not only in particular traits but also in the favorability of those traits. The typical man was seen to have 29 favorable characteristics and only 8 unfavorable ones. Ascriptions to women, in contrast, consisted of 20 favorable traits and 17 unfavorable traits. The scale of good versus bad clearly tilts in favor of men.

What are the characteristics that people see as distinguishing women and men? Generally, men are described by a series of traits that reflect competence, rationality, and assertiveness.[3] Men, for example, are viewed as independent, objective, active, competitive, adventurous, self-confident, and ambitious. Women are seen as possessing the opposite of each of these traits. They are characterized as dependent, subjective, passive, not competitive, not adventurous, not self-confident, and not ambitious. In each instance, people have indicated that the trait the male possesses is the more desirable trait for someone in our Western culture. Women are not seen as all bad, however. There is a cluster of positively valued traits that people see as more typical of women than men; these traits generally reflect warmth and expressiveness. Women are described as tactful, gentle, aware of the feelings of others, and able to express tender feelings easily. Men in contrast are viewed as blunt, rough, unaware of the feelings of others, and unable to express their own feelings. Yet while women are credited with a number of positive traits, the numbers are still less. Furthermore, some good things may be better than others, and, in a competitive society such as ours, competence seems to be a more highly valued trait than warmth.

One of the clearest demonstrations of these differences in favorability was provided by Inge Broverman and her colleagues.[4] These investigators asked practicing mental health clinicians (clinical psychologists, psychiatrists, and psychiatric social workers) to complete a sex-role questionnaire after being given one of three possible sets of instructions. In one case, the clinicians were asked to "think of normal, adult men" and then to indicate which adjectives would be most indicative of a "mature, healthy, socially competent adult man." A second group of clinicians was given similar instructions, except that "woman" was used instead of "man" in the description. Finally, a third group was asked to complete the same questionnaire, but this time in terms of a mature, healthy, socially competent adult *person.* The results of this study were striking, although a bit depressing for some of us. As in most of the stereotyping studies, male and female judges showed substantial agreement, suggesting that stereotypes are indeed shared by the culture as a whole. More importantly, there was very high agreement between those traits judged characteristic of the adult man and those used to describe the adult person. Healthy persons were described as competent, independent, and objective, and healthy men were pictured the same way. Women, in contrast, were seen as quite different from the healthy adult person, embodying the "less healthy" characteristics of emotionality, conceit, and submissiveness. Apparently, some clinicians feel that what is healthy for a person in general may be very unhealthy for a woman.

This same brand of bias can be found in other areas of activity as well. Using a method similar to that of Broverman, Virginia Schein asked male management personnel in insurance companies to describe either women, men, or successful middle-level managers.[5] Once again, differences were apparent. These male managers described "men" and "successful middle-level managers" in very similar terms, while "women" were seen as quite different from the successful manager.

The evidence from these studies suggests that the existence of sex-related stereotypes is more than a case of equal but different. Heterogeneity could, after all, be a good thing, and many people would agree with the frequently stated "Vive la difference," as applied to the sexes. But can we wish a long life to these perceived differences when they imply not only that men and women are different but also that what is associated with males is better? Perhaps the danger of stereotyping is that it so often involves such assumptions of better and worse.

DEVIATING FROM THE STEREOTYPE

While male-associated traits are often viewed as preferable, both men and women may be negatively evaluated when they deviate from the expectations for their sex. In one demonstration of the consequences of deviation, Jeanne Marecek asked college students to evaluate the problems of a patient in therapy.[6] These hypothetical patients were described in brief vignettes, which included the age and sex of the patient and some comments that the patient made to the therapist. These comments served as the major experimental manipulation in the study, in addition to the sex of the patient, and provided evidence of either aggressive or dependent behavior of the patient toward the therapist. On the basis of this information, the students were asked to judge the seriousness of the patient's psychiatric problem. As expected, men who expressed dependency toward the therapist were rated as having far more serious problems than women who expressed the same level of dependency. In a parallel fashion, women who expressed aggression were seen as more disturbed than men who did so.

In this instance, both of the behaviors that deviate from the stereotype are fairly negative. Dependency, for example, is a characteristic that is viewed as both feminine and undesirable. Aggression can also have negative connotations. In terms of these undesirable behaviors, deviating from the stereotype seems to result in less positive evaluations of either the man or woman who deviates. Do similar evaluations result when the deviation occurs on more positive characteristics?

Social psychologists Janet Spence, Robert Helmreich, and Joy Stapp have conducted a set of studies in which people are asked to evaluate both men and women who are acting in ways somewhat inconsistent with sex-role stereotypes.[7] Let's first consider their basic procedure. Subjects are asked to watch a videotaped presentation of a male or a female college student being interviewed for a position as freshmen orientation advisor. During the interview, the applicant is asked a number of questions about his or her academic background, future professional plans, and general hobbies and interests. By carefully constructing the scripts of these interviews, Spence and her colleagues were able to provide subjects with information about two specific characteristics of the applicant—the general level of competence and the masculine or feminine nature of the applicant's interests. Competent applicants revealed during the course of the interview that they had an A-average in their college courses, planned to pursue graduate work, and had successfully participated in a number of extracurricular activities. The incompetent applicant described himself or herself as having struggled to maintain a C average, having limited career plans, and having tried out for a few activities in college but generally bombing out in the attempt. The second variation in the scripts concerned the interests of the applicant. Masculine applicants were portrayed as physics majors, and their interests included reading history and biography, Red Cross lifesaving, and sports cars. Feminine applicants described themselves as majoring in interior and fashion design, and their hobbies included bridge, gourmet cooking, art, and the college glee club. Thus, each subject in this experiment viewed either a male or a female who was either competent or incompetent and who had either masculine or feminine interests.

The design of this study is rather complicated, but the basic findings are clear and can be summarized quite easily. First of all, subjects generally preferred a competent applicant to an incompetent applicant, regardless of the applicant's sex or interests. Such a finding is hardly surprising, since there is an abundance of evidence within the area of interpersonal attraction, suggesting that the incompetents of the world are not particularly loved. A second strong finding was that applicants with masculine interests were liked better than applicants with feminine interests, whether the applicant was a male or a female. Thus, while the woman who deviated from typically feminine interests was rated positively, the man who did not show expected masculine interests was not evaluated as favorably. In some ways, this finding is not surprising, given the mountains of evidence showing that masculine characteristics are generally viewed more positively than feminine characteristics. On the other hand, it does seem a bit surprising that the woman who is deviating from the feminine stereotypical role in taking on masculine activities is preferred to the more stereotypical female. To add to the unexpected nature of this finding, the authors also collected information about the subject-judges' own attitudes toward women's roles and were able to classify subjects as being traditional, moderate, or liberal in their attitudes toward the appropriate roles for women. Traditionals are defined as those who are conservative in their view, favoring more limited roles for women, more submission to the man, and less equality in work and social spheres. Liberals, in contrast, show greater agreement with the movement toward women's equality and with changes in traditional sex-role standards. The surprising finding is that subjects in each of these three groups continued to view the competent woman with masculine interests more favorably than the other women.

How do we explain these findings? The most obvious explanation would be that women who deviate from the stereotyped role are not disliked, as long as the deviation is toward a positive characteristic. (Some evidence from the study suggests that if women are incompetent in a masculine activity, they may be more strongly disliked.) If masculine activities are generally considered better, then anyone who can cut it at that level is considered good. Another factor that may enter into the picture is that subjects actually saw the person they were evaluating. In this case, the young woman who described herself as having masculine interests was a rather attractive, likable college student. Being able to see her would prevent subjects from assuming that a woman who would be interested in such activities must also be ugly, bitchy, and of questionable female appearance. (While such labels may sound extreme, we know that people will infer a whole realm of characteristics given limited information about another person, and, for a woman who deviates from the normative role, such attributions are not unlikely though perhaps less extreme than I have depicted.) Furthermore, while the young woman in question expressed some masculine interests, she did not deny any interests in the roles of motherhood and family, which may be more central to the woman's stereotype. Other research has, in fact, shown that when women express opinions that counter these central feminine values they are liked less than a more traditional woman.[8]

But there is another explanation for these findings, which centers on the question of whether subjects were being honest in their responses. While it may be comforting to think that the woman who is competent in masculine endeavors has become accepted in our society, a glance around the society can cause some doubt as to whether such changes have really occurred. Perhaps subjects, when asked to complete a questionnaire immediately after viewing the applicant, respond in a fairly superficial manner that doesn't reflect their true beliefs. Yet if these same subjects were given additional time to process the information they have just seen and to organize it in the context of their basic beliefs, would the same liberality be seen?

To answer this question, Spence and her colleagues asked some subjects to write open-ended comments about the videotaped applicant before they responded to the standardized questionnaire.

In this format, the authors felt that subjects might feel freer to formulate their impressions. Subsequently, when these people filled out the standard questionnaire, their answers might reflect their real impressions to a greater extent than would the responses of subjects who went immediately to the questionnaire. These procedures did produce changes in the evaluations of the student applicant. While competent people were still preferred to incompetent people, the subjects showed changes in their views of the masculinity and femininity of the applicant. Only those women who were favorable toward the women's movement continued to like the masculine competent woman more than the feminine competent woman. Conservative women and *both* liberal and conservative males now favored the woman who was competent in a feminine sphere to one who pursued more masculine activities.

Interestingly, there were very few changes in subjects' evaluations of the male applicant as a function of the intervening description. In both conditions, subjects liked competent males more than incompetent males and those males who engaged in masculine activities more than those who engaged in feminine activities.

I have devoted considerable space to this study because I think it is an important offering to the study of stereotypes. Conceptions of men and women and of masculinity and femininity do differ, and the evidence is virtually unanimous in showing that masculinity is more valued in our society. Furthermore, while some would suggest that the stereotypes are changing, more careful consideration suggests that these changes may be only skin-deep. The underlying beliefs may remain unaltered despite the surface responses to a psychologist's questionnaire.

WHY STEREOTYPES?

There are a number of explanations for the source of stereotyped views of men and women. One possible reason is that stereotypes reflect reality—that men are viewed as more independent because men in general *are* more independent and that women are seen as more passive because women in general *are* more passive than men. This basis for stereotypes has been termed the "kernel of truth." It is argued that stereotypes develop from real differences that exist among groups, although often the stereotype is exaggerated far beyond its original kernel. Later on, we'll look at many areas of behavior in which men and women do differ. In some cases, the stereotyped beliefs will be seen to reflect the normative patterns of men and women in our society. In other instances, however, the evidence will show that the beliefs are quite inaccurate. Why would such beliefs persist if they are not true? In part, the answer is that we are selective in our perception: we tend to see confirmation of what we believe and to avoid seeing that which contradicts our beliefs. Beyond that bias, there seems to be a tendency in our society to emphasize group differences. Perhaps in part because of social scientists, we often concentrate more intently on locating the differences among people rather than the similarities. Anthropologists have become aware of what is termed the "exotic bias," which predisposes the outside observer to look at ways in which another culture differs from our own and to ignore ways in which that culture is the same. A similar bias may operate as we consider men and women: they look different, and so they must be different.

Beyond these distortions of judgment, however, there are other influences that strengthen our assumptions that all men are one way and all women are another. The media, for example, present many examples of men and women, and analyses of these presentations have often shown the pictures to be quite one-dimensional. A number of investigators have looked at children's readers, for example, and the results of these studies are consistent.[9] Boys are seen as active, curious, and independent; girls are portrayed as dependent, showing little curiosity or initiative, and needing the help of boys. Men are shown actively solving problems and going off to work, while women are shown in the kitchen, waiting for the father to come home to make important decisions. It is undoubtedly true that these characteristics accurately describe some boys and girls and some men and women. The argument, however, is whether the stories show the range of alternatives that men and women do exhibit in real life. Many more women work, for example, than one would guess by reading children's books, and many more girls are active and playing rough than the readers indicate. Similarly, some boys sit quietly and read, and some fathers change diapers. Yet by focusing on the more stereotyped aspects of men and women, the readers may perpetuate these beliefs.

Television and magazines also make their contributions. Social psychologists Leslie McArthur and Beth Resko systematically analyzed the roles of men and women in television commercials, and the differences were abundant.[10] First of all, there were more men than women shown in the commercials. More interesting, however, were the differences in the kinds of roles that men and women played in these commercials. Of the men, 70% were shown as authorities—people who had the facts about the product in question —while only 14% of the females who were central figures in the commercials were shown in this role. In contrast, the role of product user, agreeing to buy or try or use the product, was primarily a female role—86% of the women were shown in this role, while only 30% of the men were shown as product users. The commercials also showed men and women getting different payoffs for using Product *X*. Men who tried the product were promised social and career advancement; women, on the other hand, were told that either their family or men in general would like them if they bought the product.

In a study of magazine articles, investigators have found similar evidence of stereotyped presentations.[11] Analysis of both fiction and nonfiction articles in a series of popular magazines showed that women continued to be portrayed as housewives in the majority of articles. Only 7% of women characters were described as married working women, which is a considerable bias when we consider that in real life more than 20 million women in this country are both working and married. Perhaps of greater impact is the fact that this same study showed that very little is changing. In a comparison of articles written in 1957 and those written in 1972, almost no differences were found, suggesting that the stereotypes are rather strongly resisting the changing realities.

Another source of stereotypes may be found in the general socialization process, which, though differing among specific families, cultures, and classes, tends to reflect the general values of the society. Although we're not dealing at any length with the socialization process in this book, an argument can certainly be made that parents and other socializing agents convey certain expectations to their children as to what grown-up men and women are like. These impressions may form the basis of stereotypes that are found much later in life.

ARE STEREOTYPES CHANGING?

Much of the evidence presented by Broverman and by Spence and Helmreich would argue against concluding that any large dents have been made in the stereotyped conceptions of men and women. While some investigators argue and present data suggesting that college students are becoming more favorable in their judgments of the average woman and are less prone to overvalue the average man,[12] other investigators find very few differences in stereotypes during the past ten years. This lack of change is especially evident when precautions are taken to minimize the pressure on subjects to respond in socially appropriate ways. It is difficult to determine what the stereotypes really are during this period. Because there is so much talk and controversy about the roles of men and women in society, people may be reluctant to voice their true beliefs when a psychologist asks them to describe the typical man or the typical woman. What experimenters call *demand characteristics* may be operating: people will say what they think the investigator wants them to say rather than what they really believe. For example, in a recent study Virginia O'Leary and Charlene Depner found that men who were asked to describe their ideal woman portrayed a virtual wonderwoman.[13] Their ideal was seen to be more competent, more successful, and more adventurous than the woman's ideal man, which has typically been (and continues to be) a highly competent figure. Although it is certainly possible that men indeed view this superwoman as the ideal, it seems more likely that some demand characteristics are operating. To avoid being labeled a chauvinist pig, men may be overstating the case.

Yet while much evidence suggests that general stereotypes have not been drastically altered, other evidence points to specific factors that do lead to a modification of stereotypes. If a person's mother has worked, for example, that person tends to have a less stereotyped view of women.[14] Both men and women whose mothers have been employed tend to see very little difference between men and women in terms of warmth and expressiveness. Furthermore, daughters of employed mothers see women as more competent than do daughters of more traditional homemakers. (However, men's judgments of competence are not altered by a working mother.) In light of the fact that increasing numbers of women are working outside the home, we might expect that the changes observed in these studies would continue to develop.

While simple awareness of the controversy may not lead people to alter their stereotyped views, actual experience with different models of men and women may have a strong effect. If children are able to view their mother in a competent working role and to see their father expressing warmth and sharing household duties, stereotypes may change. Similarly, changes in the images of men and women presented in magazines, in books, and on television may also lead to altered views of men and women in future years. For now, however, we must conclude that stereotypes are still alive and doing reasonably well in our culture.

Chapter 3

Stereotypes of Women and Men: Performance Evaluation

All the pursuits of men are the pursuits of women also,
but in all of them a woman is inferior to a man.

Plato

Plato's statement may offer comfort to proponents of male superiority, but it must be discouraging to large segments of the population. Although Plato was preaching this doctrine several thousand years ago, there are many current-day advocates of the view that women are inferior in all pursuits.

In the previous chapter, we considered the personality characteristics that people tend to ascribe to women and men in our society. As we saw, people have a rather clear image of what men and women are like, and the individual who deviates from this stereotyped picture may be considered less attractive or less likable than the image-matching man or woman. In this chapter, we'll deal with one of the ramifications of these stereotypes—how the performance of a man or woman is evaluated.

You might think that the evaluation of a specific performance would be an objective process, judged on characteristics of the performance itself rather than on assumptions about the personality or ability of the performer. Yet performance judgment is rarely a totally objective process. Two people may view the same event and interpret it differently. In the same way, it is possible for someone to view two people acting in exactly the same way and yet come to different conclusions about that behavior. Consider a magician and a psychic. If you were to watch a magician cause a coin to bend, you would probably figure that some trick was involved. Perhaps the coin was made of rubber, or maybe the magician switched coins at some point without your noticing. Now consider a psychic causing a similar coin to bend. If you were a true believer in psychic powers, you would probably not feel that a trick had been played on you, but instead you would see the demonstration as proof of the power of psychic phenomena.

In much the same way, people shade their views of the performance of men and women. Equipped with stereotypic beliefs about what men and women are like and what men and women can do, we tend to view actual behavior in a way that fits our stereotypic beliefs. In most cases, the result of this biased judgment process is a devaluation of women, although as we shall see there are some important exceptions.

EVALUATING PERFORMANCE

In an early demonstration of sex-linked biases, a psychologist named Philip Goldberg gave a group of women several articles to read.[1] The articles were scholarly discussions, such as might appear in professional journals, and dealt with a variety of topics: architecture, dietetics, law, and city planning. The women were asked to read these articles and to judge how good they were: how scholarly, well-written, and so on. There was one catch, however. Some of the women read an article that was written by John McKay, while others read the same article with the author identified as Joan McKay. Given the evidence of the article, would the author's name make a difference? Yes. In every case, the article authored by a man was rated more favorably than the same article authored by a woman. Apparently, the assumption that men are superior led people to view the same objective evidence in different ways, depending on the sex of the author.

Goldberg concluded that women are prejudiced against women, and other investigators who have replicated this particular study have demonstrated that men are prejudiced against women too.[2] Clearly, the prospects are rather discouraging for the woman who wants to be evaluated favorably for her work, even when she chooses a typically feminine field such as dietetics in which to work.

One ray of hope emanates from Israel. Harriet Mischel suggested that while such biases can be seen in the United States, where sex roles are still relatively rigid, a less sex-typed society might not show the same biases.[3] Israel has adopted a policy of equality between the sexes that is far more flexible than that of the United States (which in turn is more liberal than many other societies). Women in Israel, for example, are required to do military service in the same way that men are and can be seen on the battlefield as well as in office jobs. If this equalization is real, then it might be reasonable to assume that the biases against women would be less. Using Israeli students as subjects in an experiment patterned after Goldberg, Mischel found that little bias was shown. While the students still tended to think of some occupations as being primarily held by males and others as being primarily held by females, these students did not bias their judgments of the male or female writer in any of the fields.

While Mischel's study suggests that the tendency to devalue the performance of women is not universal, it seems likely that her subjects represent an exception rather than the norm. Numerous other studies have provided evidence that, when the woman is described as having the same credentials as does a man, she will be rated lower in competence, recommended for a lower position within the organizational structure, and hired less frequently.[4] Such differences in the judgment process are of interest not only to the social scientist. There are important implications for social policy as well, and in recent years considerable pressure has been exerted to eliminate these biases in employment and education.

SOME EVIDENCE OF EQUALITY

Yet the picture for women is not totally bleak. In some instances, the woman may be evaluated as favorably for her performance as is a man. The necessary ingredient appears to be the recognition by some authority of the performance in question: if some recognized critic or judge puts a seal of approval on the woman's work, then most observers seem willing to evaluate the woman's work in a positive manner. In a demonstration of this equalization process, Gail Pheterson, Sara Kiesler, and Philip Goldberg showed undergraduate students examples of artwork, presumably painted by either a male or a female artist.[5] In some cases, subjects were told that the painting was simply an entry in a local art competition, and with this information subjects showed the familiar tendency to consider the male artist more talented than the female artist. In another condition, the authors said that the painting had been declared the contest winner. With this legitimacy, subjects rated the male and the female painter identical in their skill.

The fact that this equalization occurred when a judge's decision was known probably reflects an important feature of performance judgment. Quality is often ambiguous. The merit of a professional article or the artistic quality of a painting is a difficult judgment to make in the abstract, particularly when a person is not highly trained in that area. To the extent that the performance is somewhat ambiguous, stereotypes may play a much more important role in the process of reaching a decision. Uncertain as to how good a painting is, we may fall back on our belief that men are generally better artists than are women. However, when we have clear proof that a painting is good (for example, when a presumably qualified judge awards it first prize), then we may be able to overcome our stereotypes and trust the evidence that we have before us. This reasoning would also suggest that the more clearly the criteria for a performance are stated, the less likely biases are to intervene in the judgment process.

In such cases, men and women may be evaluated equally for equivalent performances.

In some cases, women may be rated even more favorably than men for their performance. To understand why this difference would occur, let's briefly consider a social-psychological model called *equity theory*.[6] According to equity theory, people prefer to experience a balance in performance situations. A person who puts more work into a job should get more payoff (for example, a larger paycheck). A person who invests less time, or effort, or talent should also be rewarded less for his or her performance. In one particular development of this theory, Gerald Leventhal and James Michaels have suggested that people who perform well in spite of a handicap will be over-rewarded for their actions.[7] As an example, a young man who is five feet tall and clears a height of 5'10" in the high jump would be considered more deserving than a six-foot-tall jumper who clears the same height. Leventhal and Michaels suggest that because the short jumper is operating under an involuntary handicap (he can't help the fact that he is small), his performance will be viewed more positively than will the leap of our six-foot-tall jumper, and he will in turn be rewarded more for his performance.

Janet Taynor and I suspected that a similar thought process might occur if people were asked to judge the performance of a woman who performed unusually well in a situation where only men are expected to excel. To test this hunch, we developed a rather detailed story involving either a man or a woman on an elevator with a holdup man.[8] In this written scenario, a gunman robs an elevator passenger and then escapes through a parking lot, warning the passenger not to follow. The story describes the passenger as acting very effectively in this emergency situation: watching which direction the gunman runs, remembering details of his appearance, and giving the police sufficient information so that they are able to apprehend the criminal quickly. The police praise the passenger for his or her effective and quick action in the emergency.

We asked undergraduate students to read one of two versions of this story, which were identical except for the sex of the passenger. After students had read the scenario, they were asked to evaluate the passenger and, in particular, to judge how deserving the passenger was of reward for his or her performance in the emergency. The situation was clearly an atypical one, and earlier ratings had established that most people thought that kind of performance was more typical of males. How did people evaluate the woman in this situation? In accord with our predictions, the woman was seen as *more* deserving of reward than the man who did the same things.

Thus, like the short high jumper, the woman, who is presumably handicapped by her sex in a situation calling for emergency action, is over-rewarded for her performance. We suspect that two ingredients are necessary for this over-reward process to occur. First, the situation must be one in which women are not expected to be able to perform like a man so that the negative expectation becomes a perceived handicap on the part of the woman. Second, it is likely that, as in the earlier study by Pheterson and her colleagues, some judgment by an authority is necessary so that the performance can't be misinterpreted. In other words, it must be clear that the performance is of high caliber.

While these studies show that it is not impossible for the woman to receive a fair (or more than fair) evaluation, the requirements for such equal evaluation are rather stringent. Unfortunately, situations in life often lack these specific characteristics. Many times we are asked to evaluate people without having any definite criteria for success or failure. We must define for ourselves what is good or bad or excellent or atrocious, and in these judgments the bias against women persists.

ATTRIBUTING CAUSES FOR PERFORMANCE

So far we have considered only the global evaluations that are made about a performance—how good the performance is and whether it is deserving of praise or criticism. Beyond this general judgment of good or bad, people may also try to explain *why* a person's performance results in a particular outcome. This general process is one that social psychologists term the *attribution process.* Basically, the assumption is made that most people like to find an explanation for things that happen around them. If you were at a horse race and had placed a $10 bet on a horse that you thought was a sure winner, what would you do when it came in last? Many people in this situation would try to find a reason for the loss. Perhaps the horse wasn't feeling well that day; maybe the jockey did something dumb; maybe another rider crowded your favorite out at the first turn. Your explanation may or may not be correct, but the essential point is that the explanation makes the event understandable to you. This explanation process is of course not limited to losing horse races. We try to find explanations for people's behavior as well, in a variety of behavioral situations.

Fritz Heider first developed attribution theory, framing it in terms of what he called a "naïve, common-sense psychology."[9] In analyzing the actions of another person, Heider suggested that a person can use internal or external explanations for the event. Internal (or personal) explanations rely on characteristics of the individual actor. For example, a person who does well on an exam may have a lot of brains and ability, or perhaps the person studied very hard. Both of these explanations would rely on traits of the actor. External (or situational) explanations that could be used would include deciding that the test had been an extremely easy one or that the person was just lucky. These explanations rely on factors outside of the individual to explain the event.

In part, our choice of explanations is influenced by prior beliefs about the person or event involved. If, for example, a friend of yours has always received A's on exams, you would probably credit another high exam score to your friend's ability—a characteristic inherent in your friend. On the other hand, if your friend always flunked exams, an unexpected A would be more likely to be attributed to external factors such as chance or an unusually easy test. Or perhaps you would decide that on this one occasion your friend had crammed extremely hard. This latter explanation would be internal (it was due to characteristics of your friend) but less permanent than ability.

The sex of the performer seems to be important in understanding what kinds of explanations people will use. Let's consider one experiment in some detail to illustrate this process. As a subject, you enter a social-psychology laboratory, and the experimenter explains that you will be asked to evaluate the performance of another student. While you won't actually meet that student, you will be able to hear his or her voice by means of headphones. The experimenter explains that the other student will be doing a perceptual task, which will involve the recognition of objects presented on blurred slides. For each slide presentation, the student will be guessing which of two possible objects is actually shown on the slide. You, as the scorekeeper, do not actually see the slides, but you have an answer sheet in front of you with the correct answers circled. The experimenter tells you to listen to the student, mark the questions that are answered correctly, and attend to any other cues in the student's voice that may help you in evaluating the performance. You then hear the student answer each of the 25 items on the test, and when you total up the score you find that your partner has answered 19 questions correctly. The experimenter then asks you to evaluate your partner's performance by answering a series of questions. These questions ask for a judgment of the performance ("How good was it?") as well as the *causes* of that performance.

In this experiment by myself and Tim Emswiller,[10] there were two major independent variables: the sex of the student performer and the sex-linkage of the task. In some cases, the student being evaluated was a male, while in other cases she was a female. In addition, the content of the task was varied. In some cases, the items were stereotypically masculine objects such as wrenches and tire jacks, and in other cases more feminine objects like colanders and whisks were listed on the answer sheets. By varying the sex of both the performer and the task, we hoped to learn more about the judgment of behavior that is either consistent or inconsistent with prevailing stereotypes.

The questionnaire that subjects filled out asked for several different judgments of the performance, but the major question of interest dealt with the perceived causes of the performance. Specifically, we asked subjects to judge how much the person's performance was "mainly due to skill" or was "mainly due to luck." How did our real subjects respond to this question? When the task was a masculine one, subjects explained the performance of the male student by skill while viewing the woman's performance as more due to luck. Despite identical evidence, subjects found different explanations for the performance of men and women (thus justifying the subtitle of this particular report: "What is skill for the male is luck for the female").

If men are accorded more skill on a masculine task, then we might expect the reverse to be true on a feminine task: women should be seen as having more skill, while men would be rated luckier. However, our results did not show this kind of balance. Women were seen as a bit more skillful and men somewhat less skillful, when subjects judged the outcome of a feminine task. Yet neither judgment was as extreme as was true on the masculine task. Overall, our results point to a greater tendency to invoke ability for a man and luck for a woman.

Had I any cause to doubt that this artificial laboratory environment reflected life in the real world, my fears were soon put to rest. Shortly after completing this study, I was sitting in a local pub with a friend (who, not incidentally, was male). To exercise our competitive spirits, we began to play an electric dart game. Basically, the game involved releasing a button at the appropriate time so that the electric representation of a dart would hit the bull's-eye. At the end of the first game, I had a clear victory with a score of 45 to 20. After winning another game, I decided to explain my winning strategy to my friend, and the result was his 40 to 20 victory on the third game. (I explained my low score on the third game by boredom.) At this point, two sweet-looking old ladies at the next table offered their interpretation of the events, speaking at an easily overheard volume. "You see," the one woman explained, "he knows how to play it but she doesn't." Unwilling to let this explanation go unchallenged, I gently explained to the woman that I had in fact won the first two games, and my nonchauvinist friend pointed out that I had taught him the "winning secret." Undaunted, the lady informed me that I had just been lucky, and I gave up, knowing that my research was valid even if my competence was still in question.

WHEN LUCK IS NOT ENOUGH

Yet surely the success of a woman is not always attributed to luck. Remember that in the Deaux and Emswiller study the task involved deciding which of two alternatives was correct. In such a situation, it is reasonable that luck might account for some people's success, even if it can't realistically explain every woman's performance on such a task. But what of situations where luck is an unlikely explanation for anyone? For example, what if you learn that Dr. Marcia Greer has finished medical school, completed an internship and residency in surgery, and set up a successful medical practice in Santa Clara, California. Would luck be an explanation that you would offer for her success? Probably not. Few people would believe that the successful work of several years could be adequately explained by a casual "She was just lucky."

Shirley Feldman-Summers and Sara Kiesler conducted an experiment in which subjects were asked to attribute causes for the success of either Dr. Marcia Greer or Dr. Mark Greer.[11] They found that luck was not often used to explain the success of either the male or female doctor. However, the explanations offered by subjects did differ as a function of the doctor's sex and as a function of the subject's sex as well. In this case, men were more likely to show bias in their judgments than were women. The male subjects in this study attributed more ability to Dr. Mark Greer than to Dr. Marcia Greer, thus supporting the earlier results of Deaux and Emswiller. In addition, these men offered two other reasons for the woman doctor's success: she had an easier task, and she tried harder. The female subjects in this particular study agreed that the woman had tried harder, but they did not view her task as easier. In contrast, they felt that the woman doctor's job was more difficult than the man's. These results suggest that luck will not always be used to explain a woman's success, though ability still seems to be firmly established as a male virtue. Before reflecting on the consequences of these differences, let's consider one more study that looked at causal attributions for failure as well as for success.

A group of Australian high school girls was asked to explain either the success or failure of a postgraduate student in one of several occupational specialties.[12] The student, as you might expect, was described as either a male or a female, and the occupations included medicine, teaching, and nursing. In general, the findings were similar among the professions, though the differences in judgment were strongest when the student was in medical school. In this case, the subjects attributed the male student's success to greater ability, while the woman's success was more strongly ascribed to good luck, an easy course, and cheating on exams! Failure conditions caused a different set of explanations to be used. Here the woman's failure was explained by a lack of ability and a lack of hard work to a greater degree than was the man's, while subjects endorsed the possibility that an unfair allegation of cheating had caused the man's failure.

Although there are some variations among these studies, each study points to differences in the explanations given for the performance of women as opposed to men. And despite the variation, there is a detectable pattern in these causal explanations that ties back to the stereotyped beliefs about men and women. As we have seen earlier, people believe men are more competent. Consequently, success by a man tends to be expected, and these successes are most often explained by invoking the inherent, stable characteristic of ability. In contrast, success by a woman seems to be less expected, and internal causes are assumed less often. Good luck, an easy task, or even cheating are circumstantial explanations used to explain the woman's success. Yet on other occasions, particularly when such external explanations are improbable, observers do credit the woman's success to some characteristic of the woman herself. She tried harder, but still she is not seen as having the same degree of ability. Under failure conditions, the available evidence suggests that just the opposite pattern occurs. For the woman, failure is seen as internally caused, the result of her own inability, while more external explanations are sought for the man's failure (such as an unfair allegation of cheating).

These differences in causal explanations may have important consequences. For example, if you believe that a person's success is due to ability, you would be more confident in offering that person a job or putting the person in charge of a difficult project. In contrast, if you believe the person simply lucked out on one occasion, you would probably not have any great confidence in the person's future success. Thus, just as stereotypes may affect performance judgments, so the explanations of these performances may affect future behaviors that can perpetuate the stereotypes of women and men.

THE MALE DILEMMA

Thus far, it seems as if most of the disadvantages of sex-role stereotyping are experienced by women. But there is another side to the coin, and from this view men are the ones who may have some reason to complain.

As we have seen, men are expected to succeed—but what if they blow it? Janet Taynor and I asked subjects to listen to a taped interview with a student who was a candidate for a prestigious scholarship program.[13] The student who did well in the interview was rated more highly if he was a male than if she was a female, consistent with other findings. But when the interview was a flop, the male applicant was seen as far more incompetent than the equivalent female candidate. Similar results were found in the study of success and failure in occupations that we discussed above. The man who succeeded was rated more positively than the woman, whether the success was in medicine, teaching, or nursing. In contrast, the man who failed in any of these fields was rated more negatively than the failing woman.[14] Thus, while evaluations of a man are more positive when success is the issue, the woman benefits (though some may argue it's a doubtful benefit) when failure is the concern. These results attest to the wisdom of Margaret Mead's observation many years ago that women are unsexed by success, while men are unsexed by failure.

Furthermore, it seems that men accrue few benefits for succeeding in a feminine field. Earlier we saw that a woman who performed well in an emergency situation could actually be over-rewarded for her performance in comparison with a man. We might then think that men could gain the same acclaim by succeeding in a woman's task, where he is assumed to have less experience or skill. Not so. In a study that parallels the gunman in the elevator, we asked subjects to evaluate a man who performed well in a situation calling for nurturant ability in relating to a small child.[15] Despite commendations from our hypothetical police, the man was not considered particularly deserving of reward. Why men don't get the same benefits for performing unexpectedly well is not clear. In part, I suspect that the activities that women typically do are considered less important than those that men do. Consequently, doing well in such unimportant situations may be no cause for reward. A related possibility is that "women's tasks" are considered easier, and thus we assume that men can do them as well as or better than women (if they so choose). Once again, however, because the job is easier, the reward may be less, and men can't gain extra points by succeeding in these arenas.

The conclusion seems to be that our rigid stereotyping has negative consequences for both sexes. Women are in trouble if they succeed, and men are in trouble if they do poorly. Our expectations for both men and women tend to limit our perspective, and as a result of our stereotyping we may too freely criticize or too sparingly praise. Ideally, the future will see some change. As we become more accustomed to viewing both men and women in a wider variety of activities, our expectations may change, and an individual's performance can be judged in its own right rather than as representative of one or the other sex.

Chapter 4

Self-Evaluations of Women and Men

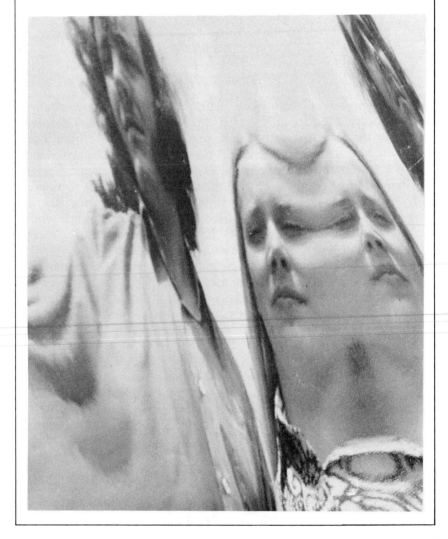

*No healthy male is ever actually modest . . . . His
conversation is one endless boast—often covert, but
always undiluted.*

H. L. Mencken

*A woman, especially if she have the misfortune of
knowing anything, should conceal it as well as she can.*

Jane Austen

In *Breakfast of Champions,* Kurt Vonnegut, Jr., tells a tale of Smart Bunny, a female rabbit who was almost like all the other wild rabbits in the forest. The one difference was that Smart Bunny had a "ballooning intellect," an intelligence as great as that of Albert Einstein. Smart Bunny worried about this difference and decided that her mind was some sort of tumor, so she hopped off to the city to have the tumor removed. Unfortunately for Smart Bunny, she was shot by a hunter on her way to tumor removal. The hunter intended to make a rabbit stew, but when he noticed Smart Bunny's large head he too decided she was diseased.

While women may not be considered diseased, the evidence in the last two chapters certainly shows that they are often viewed in a less positive light than men. But do men and women incorporate the same cultural stereotypes in evaluating themselves? Do men see themselves as competent, while women minimize their abilities? Or to put it in a less reverent way, does the intelligent woman attribute her brains to a tumor?

Psychologists have approached the question of self-evaluation in a number of ways, and we'll consider three of these approaches in this chapter: (1) general measures of self-esteem, (2) expectations for future performance, and (3) evaluations and explanations of past performance.

A VIEW OF ONESELF

Basic to most theories of personality and social development is the notion of a self-concept—the way that a person views himself or herself. Theorists have generally assumed that this concept develops early in life, though it can be modified through experience as the person grows older. Self-esteem is one particular aspect of this concept, and it is generally defined as the degree of positive or negative regard that one has for oneself.

Numerous methods have been used to measure the self-concept, but the most common approach is a simple pencil-and-paper questionnaire. These questionnaires contain items such as "I'm pretty sure of myself" or "I often question how worthwhile my life is," and subjects are asked to indicate their agreement or disagreement with each statement. People who indicate positive feelings for themselves are considered high in self-esteem, while people who indicate uncertainty or negative feelings are considered low in self-esteem.

Given the strong evidence that stereotypes of men are more favorable than stereotypes of women, we might expect that the self-concepts of men and women would reflect these same norms. Yet surprisingly, this is not the case. Studies that have compared the scores of women and men on standardized self-esteem scales generally find no difference: men and women indicate equivalent levels of self-esteem. This equality has been found for all age groups studied, from kindergarten through college.[1]

How can we explain the fact that, although society seems to value men more than women, men and women themselves have equally high self-esteem? One possible explanation is that both sexes accept the roles that they have been assigned by society. While these roles may be different, and in fact unequal, women may be as satisfied with their role as are men. Essentially, this argument would suggest that men and women compare themselves to a different standard and that self-esteem is relative to this standard, rather than an absolute measure. Thus, when a woman evaluates herself, she does so in relation to the ideal woman, while a man evaluates himself in comparison to the ideal man. One way to check this possibility would be to ask both sexes to rate their ideal selves and their actual selves. If standards are different, we should expect the ideals of men and women to differ, but the discrepancy between the ideal and the actual self should be about the same for both sexes.

Another explanation for the equality of self-esteem in men and women is a more methodological one. Some people have suggested that self-esteem scales contain two distinct types of items, which have been termed *self-acceptance* and *self-regard*.[2] Self-acceptance refers to a willingness to accept oneself as one is, despite any flaws or weaknesses, and could be more typical of women. Self-regard, in contrast, refers to a more active affirmation of one's worth and capabilities and could be more typical of males. If these two types of items were balanced within a single scale, the net result would be equal self-esteem scores for males and females, even though the two sexes might be responding positively to different items.

One other problem in comparing the self-esteem of men and women should be noted. Many times, investigators are interested in predicting the relationship between self-esteem and other types of behavior. These predictions are often derived from theories of self-concept development and suggest that people high in self-esteem should behave differently than people low in self-esteem. For example, theorists have posited that persons high in self-esteem should be more resistant to cheating, should be lower in anxiety, and should be more confident in performance situations. Yet while these predictions are generally supported in the male population, self-esteem does not seem to predict these behaviors for women.[3] It is not clear why these relationships are much stronger for men than for women. Some have suggested that women may be more responsive to situational factors than are men and that their personality dispositions have less influence in the face of other pressures. However, evidence for this contention is not strong.[4]

Another possibility is that investigators have looked primarily at situations that are relevant to the male image and not to the female image. If men and women are using different standards to judge their self-worth, then perhaps the situations investigators have chosen are closer to the male image than to the female image. We will consider the problems surrounding task selection in more detail later. For the moment, however, we must conclude that there are no differences between men and women in their overall level of self-esteem, though the basis for self-esteem may be somewhat different.

I THINK I CAN, I THINK I CAN . . .

While general measures of self-esteem reveal an equality between men and women, there are strong and consistent differences between men and women in more specific areas that relate to self-confidence. For example, if a person is asked to predict how well he or she will do on a particular task, we might expect that a person with high self-esteem would predict a better performance than someone with low self-esteem. Because we have seen that men and women score equally on self-esteem, we might therefore expect that they would predict the same levels of performance. Instead, we find that men and boys consistently predict that they will do better than do women and girls.

The basic procedure for experiments dealing with this kind of behavior is quite simple. Generally, the experimenter will describe the particular task to the subject and then will ask the subject how well he or she expects to do. This question can be phrased in either a general way (for example, "How well or how poorly do you think you will do?") or in terms specific to the task ("How many anagrams do you think you will solve?"). In nearly every instance where these procedures have been followed, men have indicated a higher expectation than have women.

The tasks that investigators have chosen for these studies have covered a wide range. Men have shown a higher expectancy for solving anagrams.[5] Men expect to do better on tests of verbal intelligence and arithmetic abilities.[6] Male college students anticipate a higher grade-point average than do women.[7] Boys surpass girls in their predictions for success in a marble-dropping game.[8] The consistency of these findings is impressive, covering a wide range of ages and tasks, and leads us to conclude that men are indeed more confident of their performance than women.

Yet while the bulk of this evidence is rather overwhelming, there are some conditions that do minimize the difference between men and women. For example, if a task is explicitly labeled feminine (even though it may be neutral), women will be a bit more optimistic in their expectations.[9] While women do not generally *exceed* men in their estimates in these situations, they do tend to match the men. Perhaps one reason for the observed differences in expectancies between men and women again lies in the tasks that have been chosen. Tasks that are less individualistic and more interpersonal might show higher estimates by women. For example, would men or women predict a higher performance if the situation required a person to offer comfort to someone who was depressed? Situations such as these have not been studied, and we can only speculate on what differences might be found.

The differences observed in expectancies may also relate back to the distinction that was made concerning self-esteem scores. Self-acceptance, as one component of self-esteem, may simply imply satisfaction with oneself, and people high on this component would not necessarily aspire to high performance nor expect to do exceptionally well. On the other hand, the definition of self-regard suggests that these kinds of aspirations are present. If men and women do differ in these two components of self-esteem, then the expectancy differences may be understandable.

Before leaving this section, we should consider the question of accuracy. Are men generally overestimating their ability and/or are women underestimating theirs? The evidence, while sparse, suggests that both patterns are true. For example, when a group of college students was asked to estimate the grades that they would receive the following term, men said they would do as well as or better than they had done the previous term, while women thought they would not do quite as well as they had in the past.[10] Actual grades for the following semester showed no difference between the men and women. Furthermore, while both sexes were less than accurate in their estimates, men had the greater margin of error. Over a five-year period, men's overestimates were substantially greater than women's underestimates. We might think that if men overestimate more than women underestimate, then the men would experience more of a letdown when their performance did not meet their expectations. As we shall see in the next few pages, however, men don't necessarily experience this disconfirmation.

THE SELF-EVALUATION YARDSTICK

In a wide variety of situations, men think they will do better than women. Yet in the majority of these same situations, men and women do equally well. Men and women are, for example, equally proficient in solving anagrams and attain the same grade-point averages in college. Despite this equality of performance, different expectations persist, and it is reasonable to ask why.

One major reason is that men *think* they have done better than women do. As we pointed out earlier, many situations lack clear-cut criteria as to what is a good performance. While we can often say whether something is pretty good or pretty bad, the finer discriminations are often subjective rather than objective. In playing golf, you know what par is and you know just where your score rates in relation to that. But what if you solve 19 out of 25 anagrams? Or you lead a group discussion? Without additional information as to what other people have done, you would probably be a little uncertain as to just how good your performance really is.

Many situations, both inside and outside the psychology laboratory, require subjective estimates of performance. And in most of these situations, we find that men feel they have done better than women feel they have, although both may have solved 19 out of 25 anagrams. Men not only expect to do better, but they believe they have done better. While this seems to be a fairly general trend, our own research suggests that the difference between men and women is most noticeable when a bad performance is at issue. Confronted with failure, women are much more likely to downgrade their performance than are men. One can argue that women are more realistic than men, in that they are willing to call a failure a failure. Men in contrast seem reluctant to acknowledge a lack of success, even though the evidence may be strong. Yet while women may have reality on their side, the consequences of this reality can be detrimental. More easily convinced that they have "blown it," women may be less willing to try again and will select themselves out of the running.

Women devalue their own performance in other ways as well. In the preceding chapter, we saw that observers explain the performance of men and women differently. Men are credited with ability when they succeed, while failures are attributed to external circumstances. For women, these patterns are nearly reversed. It may come as no surprise to learn that men and women also explain their own behavior differently. The experimental procedures for demonstrating this difference are similar to ones described earlier. After men and women have performed, for example, an anagram task, they are asked to respond to a series of questions that include reasons for the performance. Men who do well tend to attribute their success to ability, while women report luck as the cause of their success. At the same time, women are much more prone to claim that a lack of ability is the cause of their failure, while men rarely use this explanation.[11]

Claiming that success is due to luck gives the individual no feeling of personal accomplishment nor any strong reason to believe that luck will strike again. Thus, by their explanations, women show a reluctance to take full credit for success, while at the same time they are more willing than men to accept personal responsibility for their failure. As we have pointed out earlier, women may be more accurate than men when they claim a lack of ability as the cause of failure, but this honesty is not conducive to future performance.

As in all research, we hope that the findings in the laboratory reflect life in the world outside. My own observations have confirmed that women do indeed use luck as a reason for many successful experiences. One informal test is to listen to students when they are discussing the results of an exam. You might try this yourself and see how often "I just lucked out" comes from women versus men. I recently made a similar observation during a party in my own apartment, where one corner of a room is filled with a 1940s vintage pinball machine (and usually with a large group of people as well). When I asked the players who had been the high winner so far, a young woman was named. The winning woman quickly intervened, explaining that her success had been just lucky, as a male player continued to try for a high score.

Interestingly, women use luck not only to explain success but as one explanation for failure as well. [12] Such a consistent use of chance in accounting for performance suggests that women may view life in general as more determined by external factors than do men. There is some evidence to support such a contention. Measures of "locus of control," which attempt to distinguish between an internal and an external orientation toward life, do show some sex differences among college-age populations (but not with younger children). Men seem to be slightly more prone to see their behavior as internally caused than are women. [13] However, the differences that have been found are really quite small, often caused by only one or two questions, and the notion of a general world view seems too weak to explain the much stronger differences found in attribution patterns.

LUCK AND SKILL AT THE COUNTY FAIR

Leonard White, Elizabeth Farris, and I were intrigued by the pattern of luck attributions among women, and we wondered whether women would actually show a preference for activities in which luck could readily be used as an explanation for performance outcomes. [14] At the same time, it seemed reasonable to believe that men might seek out situations in which they could test their ability and in which ability could be claimed as a cause of any success. Our first approach to this question was to find a natural situation in which people do engage in either skill or luck activities. The midway of a county fair seemed a likely spot. Games at fairs are numerous and cover a range from those in which purely luck is involved (for example, Bingo) to those requiring more skill (such as tossing rings around Coke bottles or using a fishing pole device to upright a bottle lying on its side). As dedicated experimenters, we immersed ourselves in the crowds at summer fairs and unobtrusively observed people as they played the various fair games. Our initial hunch was correct. Games that involved some degree of skill were far more popular among the men at the fair than among the women. The women, in contrast, were more likely to engage in games of luck than in games of skill. Yet while the behavior at the fair confirmed our expectations, we were not totally convinced. Perhaps people playing the games did not see luck or skill as the critical difference. Maybe there was some other difference among these games that accounted for the choices of women and men.

Because we could not have any control over the games that were present at the fairs, we decided to set up our own fair in the laboratory. We borrowed an electric dart game (very much like the one my friend and I had played at the local pub) and then presented subjects with a choice between two supposedly different games. Subjects were told that they could play either a skill or a luck game. In the former case, the instructions stated that scores were dependent on ability and a sense of timing, while the latter game was described as purely chance, with scores determined much like those in a slot machine. In selecting between these two alternatives, our male and female college students showed a strong divergence in their choices. Nearly 75% of the men asked to play the game in which skill was required, while approximately 65% of the women said they would prefer to play the luck game.

Our results in two different situations seem quite consistent, and other observations suggest that these differences between men and women are quite pervasive. Friends who have been in Las Vegas, for example, tell me that the chance-determined slot machines are primarily used by women, while other games that are thought to require more strategy seem to be overpopulated by men. Why do these differences occur? Why do men prefer ability games while women prefer to engage in games of chance? In our laboratory study of choices, we tried to answer these questions by asking subjects to fill out questionnaires after they had made their choices. Importance of the game was not the answer. Both women and men felt it was more important to do well on a game in which skill was required. Expectancy seems to be the key. As we have seen before, men tend to expect to do better than do women in a variety of situations, and our skill game was no exception to this rule. Men thought they would do much better than did women. On the luck game, however, there was no difference between the sexes—both thought they had a moderate chance of being successful when the outcome was determined purely by chance. Yet if you look at the differences in expectancy within each sex, the reason for the choices becomes clearer. Men's estimate of success was much higher for the skill game than it was for the luck game, and thus it seems reasonable that they would select the game of skill. In contrast, because women had such a low estimate of their chances for success on the skill game, the luck game offered the greater potential for a payoff. Women saw their probabilities for success as higher on the luck game than on the skill game, and it is therefore not surprising that they chose the luck game.

Our results do not mean that women will always prefer a luck activity. If we can find a situation in which women have a reasonably high estimate of their chances for success, then we would expect that they too will choose a skill game. For example, if a situation required interpersonal skills, perhaps women would be more confident of their success when skill rather than luck was the causal factor. Yet as we saw earlier, research so far has revealed few situations in which women will show a high expectancy, and, while expectations remain low, we can expect women to prefer a luck activity.

While women certainly show a predominant tendency to invoke luck, as opposed to the use of ability by men, there are some encouraging exceptions to this pattern. For example, Daniel Bar-Tal and Irene Frieze divided women into groups on the basis of their scores on a test of achievement motivation (which we'll discuss in more detail in the next chapter).[15] They found that women who were high in a need for achievement used effort as a cause for both success and failure. Rather than relying on external reasons, these women were crediting themselves with the qualities causing success. I found a similar pattern of results in a study of men and women in first-level management positions in a number of large organizations.[16] Neither the women nor the men in these corporations felt that luck had much to do with their success. Both sexes said that effort was responsible for their successful performance, though only men believed that ability was an equally important cause. Remember that this is the same pattern we found in observers' judgments of the performance of men and women. Luck was used to explain a woman's performance when that was a possible explanation, but when a doctor's career had to be explained, observers would allow effort as a cause for the women, while ability was used for the man. Men and women themselves again seem to reflect these normative beliefs. A successful woman manager can't reasonably believe that her position is due to luck, but she uses the less stable characteristic of effort, whereas the man will invoke stable ability to explain the same behavior.

In discussing the self-evaluation processes of men and women, we have found some very consistent patterns that point to self-enhancement by men and self-deprecation by women. These terms are relative, to be sure. In terms of human honesty, it is difficult to judge whether overconfidence or underconfidence is more or less meritorious. Smart Bunny may have thought her brain was a tumor. Yet would it be less bizarre for her male rabbit counterpart to interpret a tumor as evidence of ballooning intellect? These are the kinds of questions we must continue to consider as we explore the differences between women and men.

Chapter 5

Striving for Achievement: Who's Afraid of Success?

It is highly probable that the undoubted superiority of
the male sex in intellectual and creative achievement
is related to their greater endowment of aggression . . . .
The hypothesis that women, if only given the opportunity
and encouragement, would equal or surpass the creative
achievements of men is hardly defensible.

Anthony Storr

Each step forward in work as a successful American
regardless of sex means a step back as a woman.

Margaret Mead

North America has frequently been called an achievement-oriented society. Indeed, in spending a single day in our culture, particularly the white middle-class segments of that culture, it is difficult to avoid the summons to achieve. Children from grade school through college are required to take achievement tests. Advertisements in magazines and on television stress the importance of advancing oneself and accomplishing, and Broadway shows, such as "How to Succeed in Business without Really Trying," have capitalized on the push of North Americans to move upward and onward. Not surprising then is the fact that social scientists have invested considerable energy in studying the achievement motives of individuals in this and in other societies.

Our concern with comparing the behavior of women and men finds fertile ground here as well. While the vast majority of the early literature on achievement motivation, numbering literally hundreds of studies, focused exclusively on men as the achievers par excellence (because women proved to be bugaboos to the original theoretical formulations), more recent developments in achievement motivation have, if anything, overemphasized the woman and her achievement orientation. In fact, among all the areas of research currently experiencing a feminist boom period, achievement motivation is in the forefront, providing an interesting comment on the continuing values of our society.

WHAT IS ACHIEVEMENT MOTIVATION?

In 1953, David McClelland and his associates presented the first lengthy discussion of achievement motivation.[1] As conceptualized by these authors and by Henry Murray, an earlier pioneer in personality research, the need for achievement was a desire to accomplish and to do things well, to excel and to achieve success in comparison with some standard of excellence. To measure the strength of this motive, investigators asked people to tell a short story about a picture (one or more of the Thematic Apperception Test Cards), and the stories were scored according to specified criteria. Stories that told of working toward a goal, wanting success, and feeling good about accomplishments were considered to reflect a high need for achievement; stories that ignored these concerns were scored as low in need for achievement.

These early investigators also assumed that achievement motivation could be aroused in people if the conditions were right. For example, if the experimenter stressed the relationship between the stories that subjects told and qualities of intelligence and leadership, then the achievement content of stories should increase. In studies with men, these assumptions proved to be true. For women, however, these "arousing" instructions seemed to have no effect, although the basic level of achievement motivation was no lower in women than in men.[2] In the dozens of investigations that followed, men continued to show the predicted relationships between arousal and achievement imagery, while the findings for women were contradictory and most often nonsupportive of the theory.[3]

As the theory of achievement motivation continued to develop, it is perhaps not surprising that psychologists began to focus exclusively on men to test theoretical predictions. Having established the fact that achievement motivation could be aroused by specific instructions and conditions, investigators went on to relate measures of achievement motivation to a wide variety of other behaviors. More complex conceptions of achievement motivation were also developed. For example, Atkinson and Feather proposed that two motives were necessary to understand achievement behavior.[4] The first, a hope for success, refers to the positive striving for accomplishment and achievement and is very close to the original achievement idea. Fear of failure was considered to be a second motive that operates in achievement situations. In this case, the focus is on the anxiety or threat posed by the possibility of failure. Atkinson and Feather proposed that a person's hope for success should be greater than the fear of failure in order for achievement-oriented behavior to result.[5] Using this conceptualization, achieve-ment-motivation theorists have developed an extensive body of data showing the relationship between achievement level (a combination of the two submotives) and level of aspiration, task preference, and persistence. Thus, for example, men high in achievement motivation will tend to select tasks of moderate difficulty, avoiding both the very easy tasks where no challenge is involved as well as the extremely difficult tasks where failure is almost certain. Men who score high in achievement motivation are also willing to work longer in attempting to solve a problem than are men who score low. High-achieving men generally perform better in academic settings and on a variety of intellectual tasks than do low achievers. These and other relationships have formed the foundation of achievement-motivation theory. During all of this rapid period of development, however, the nature of achievement behavior in women remained shrouded in ignorance.

DO WOMEN HAVE A NEED TO ACHIEVE?

In attempting to explain why women and men differ in their achievement behavior, investigators have developed two different arguments. One explanation says that men and women are motivated by different needs. The other explanation suggests that achievement motivation is pervasive in both men and women but that the areas in which achievement will occur simply differ. Let's briefly consider each of these positions.[6]

One way to explain the difference between men and women in their achievement behavior is to talk about two different needs that may often be in conflict with one another. Men, as this argument goes, are motivated primarily by achievement needs, but for women affiliation needs are more important. Thus, while men are striving to match or surpass some standard of excellence, women are supposedly striving for social approval. There is some evidence that supports this argument. Women, for example, generally score higher than men on scales that measure a desire for affiliation.[7] On the other hand, measures of achievement motivation show no real differences in the scores of men and women. Furthermore, there is no evidence to support the contention that women are more influenced by social reinforcement than are men. Therefore, while the affiliation-versus-achievement explanation may fit many stereotypes, experimental support for this argument is lacking.

A second interpretation of the differences between women and men assumes that both sexes have similar needs for achievement. According to this explanation, however, there is a difference in the kinds of activities and goals on which men and women focus their achievement needs. In some ways, this argument is similar to the previous one. Women, it is said, are more concerned with social skills and interpersonal successes than they are with intellectual or academic task performance. But according to this second explanation, these social areas are important for women because they represent achievement and not because they are satisfying affiliation needs or needs for social approval. Thus, men may demonstrate their achievement behavior in mechanical tasks, academic pursuits, and sports activities. Women, perhaps because of early training, may attempt to excel in social situations or in more domestic spheres. "The hostess with the mostest," according to this position, would be demonstrating the same kinds of achievement motivation as the upwardly mobile executive—only the area in which excellence was sought would differ. In my own mind, this second interpretation receives far more support from the available evidence. For example, when experimental instructions have stressed the importance of social skills, women have shown an increase in the achievement imagery of their stories but not an increase in the purely affiliative ideas. If it is only the *area* of achievement that is different for men and women, and not the *motive* itself, then we should be able to find the same general relationships between achievement motivation and other measures such as persistence among women that have been previously established for men.

It may seem that the area of achievement motivation is already quite complicated enough. Yet a doctoral student named Matina Horner added a whole new dimension to the study of achievement behavior while doing her dissertation research in 1968. Since 1968, Matina Horner has become president of Radcliffe College, and the concept she introduced—fear of success—has become a watchword both in and out of academic circles.[8] We'll spend much of the remainder of this chapter considering fear of success as it relates to the achievement behavior of both men and women.

THE MOTIVE TO AVOID SUCCESS

We have already talked about a hope for success and a- fear of failure. What Matina Horner proposed was a new concept, which she called fear of success. Horner suggested that many people, and particularly women, have a motive to avoid success because they expect negative consequences if they do succeed. For women, these negative consequences might include such feelings as being "unfeminine" or a fear of being socially rejected by men. Although some men might also be afraid of success, Horner predicted that this motive would be much more common among women than men, due to the different socialization pressures the two sexes experience. Horner also suggested that, if more women than men were shown to have this motive, then the earlier results on achievement behavior that were so inconsistent for women might be easier to explain. Both men and women might have a high need to achieve. But if women were also motivated to avoid success, then the connection between the measure of achievement motivation and subsequent behavior might be much less direct for women than for men.

To determine whether people actually are afraid of success, Horner asked a number of students at the University of Michigan to write a story, given the following sentence: "After first term finals, Anne (John) finds herself (himself) at the top of her (his) medical school class." The women students were always given the Anne sentence, and men students were given the sentence describing John. Horner then analyzed the stories students wrote, assuming, as have earlier achievement theorists, that people tell stories that indicate how they themselves feel. Stories Horner considered to indicate a motive to avoid success included those in which the character tried to deny the success, was unhappy about doing well, or had negative experiences as a result of the high grades. For example, some stories suggested that Anne decided to quit medical school and become a nurse so that her boyfriend could become the top person in the class. A more ingenious story suggested that Anne was the code name for a group of medical students who took turns taking exams under the bogus name. An even more bizarre story told of Anne's classmates becoming so disgusted with her that they took turns jumping up and down on her body.[9]

Overall, Horner found that 65% of the women she tested, but only 10% of the men, told stories that indicated a fear of success. She concluded that women are indeed more often afraid of success than men, and from this point on, the research on fear of success accelerated. The idea is a catchy one, with almost a public-relations flavor, and many have assumed that we now understand why the achievement literature was so confusing for so long. Yet before we get overconfident in our knowledge, perhaps we should look more carefully at the evidence that has accumulated since Horner's original work.

WHO'S AFRAID OF SUCCESS?

Since Horner's original study, dozens of investigators have asked men and women to tell stories about John and Anne in medical school. Depending on the time, the place, the age of the subjects, and other characteristics of the person or the situation, the percentage of men and women indicating a fear of success may vary. Yet in general, even given our more liberated times, the percentage of women showing fear of success does not seem to be decreasing very much. [10] However, although the absolute percentages have not altered radically, there is some evidence that the kinds of negative consequences that women describe may be changing. Instead of foreseeing outright rejection for success, women are more likely to describe realistic conflicts between, for example, a job and a family. [11] While such consequences are still scored as indicating a fear of success, they seem far more reasonable than a maimed body!

Showing more change than women are the men. In a recent study done at Dartmouth College, 62% of the men told stories indicating a fear of success, and a similar study at the University of Michigan reported 79% of the men with high fear-of-success stories. [12] Comparisons have also been made between blacks and whites. In one such study, fear of success was found to be higher in black men (67%) than black women (29%), just the reverse of findings for white men and women. [13] I would guess that by now members of nearly every conceivable category of people have been asked to tell stories about John and Anne. Additional investigations have been carried out seeking to find other personality and socialization variables that might relate to a person's fear-of-success score. [14] If Horner's test really does measure a person's motivation to avoid success, it would appear that a very large number of people fear success.

Yet before we assume that vast numbers of women and men are tremoring with thoughts of success, we should consider more carefully what else this test might be measuring. When people tell a story about Anne or John in medical school, are they really projecting their own motives onto the story? Or is it possible that they are simply responding to a stereotype and writing what they think an average male or an average female might do in that particular situation?

Lynn Monahan, Deanna Kuhn, and Phillip Shaver suggested that it should be possible to determine the extent to which stereotypes are operating, as opposed to "intrapsychic" motives, by asking both men and women to tell stories about both Anne and John. [15] If stereotypes are influencing people's responses, then both men and women should tell more fear-of-success stories about Anne than about John, reflecting the stereotyped belief that women find success more aversive than do men. On the other hand, if these stories really tap the individual's own motives, then we would expect that women would tell more stories indicating a fear of success about both Anne and John than would men, indicating their own stronger fears of success. The results that Monahan, Kuhn, and Shaver obtained suggest that cultural stereotypes may be the better explanation. Both men and women told substantially more stories indicating a fear of success when they were given the sentence with Anne. In fact, under these conditions, men told even more such stories (68%) than did women (51%). In contrast, only 21% of the men and only 30% of the women indicated negative incidents when they were talking about John in medical school. Other investigators have found these same kinds of differences when men and women respond to both cues,[16] and the evidence certainly suggests that the stereotype is more powerful than the motive.

While stereotyped beliefs account for a large portion of the fear-of-success stories, both men and women apparently do believe that success can have negative consequences. What are these negative consequences? And do they follow any success, or are there different kinds of success? In her original work, Horner used the single situation of medical school and made the assumption that this would be a typical situation that would arouse the basic fear-of-success motive in both men and women. Yet since then, many people have pointed out that a person can be successful in a whole variety of situations, and it is not necessary to assume that a single person would fear each situation. For example, Thelma Alper asked female nursing students to tell stories about an Anne who was at the top of her nursing class. Under these conditions, the nursing students showed far less fear of success than they did with the medical school description.[17]

Fran Cherry and I suspected that the critical factor might be the out-of-role nature of the behavior. It's not only that women anticipate some negative consequences for succeeding in the traditionally male medical school setting. Rather, we suggested, both men and women would anticipate some negative consequences when their success occurred in a nontraditional setting, and in fact there should be little difference between men and women when the situations are balanced in this way. To test this assumption, we asked both men and women to write stories about one of four possible situations. In half the cases, the situation was being top in medical school, and the principal character was either Anne or John. The other half of the time, either John or Anne was described as being at the top of the nursing school class. When we analyzed the stories the men and women told, we found that our hunch was right. While only 40% of the men indicated fear of success when writing about John in medical school, 63% of their stories about John in nursing school showed fear-of-success imagery. Among the women, 50% wrote negative stories about Anne in medical school, but only 13% described negative events when Anne was in nursing school. Both men and women responded to the stereotypes as well: 70% of the men wrote negative stories about Anne in medical school, and 65% of the women wrote negative stories about John in nursing school. [18] These results pose a serious question for those who assume that women are more afraid of success than men. Apparently, it all depends on the situation. When success occurs in a situation in which either men or women are not expected to engage, much less to succeed, then there will be negative consequences for success. The sex and the situation must be considered together.

At least people writing hypothetical stories will assume that the character would experience negative consequences. But we have not yet considered what may be the most important question about the fear of success—do the stories that people tell have any relationship to actual behavior? Does someone who writes a story about the negative consequences of success actually avoid success in a real-life situation?

DO THOSE WHO FEAR SUCCESS AVOID SUCCESS?

In her original dissertation work, Matina Horner was concerned with the connection between a person's fear-of-success motive (as measured by the story he or she told) and that person's behavior in competitive situations. Horner predicted that people who had a high fear of success would perform more poorly in a competitive situation than would people who did not fear success. Although her own work found only weak support for this prediction among women and no support among men, a later study by Vivian Makosky shows that fear-of-success scores may predict competitive behavior for women. [19] Makosky conducted an experiment using women college students who were either high or low on fear of success as measured by the stories they told about Anne in medical school. All the subjects were asked to work on the same anagram task. However, half of the women were told that the task was a feminine one and that women generally do better than men, while the other half of the subjects were told that the task was masculine and that men generally do better than women. In addition, Makosky set up three different conditions of competition. In some cases the woman was competing against a man, in some cases she was competing against another woman, and in other cases there was no competition at all, since the subject simply worked on the anagrams alone. Makosky found that women who were not afraid of success performed best when they were competing against a man or when the task had been labeled a masculine task. In contrast, women who were high on fear of success did better when they were competing against a woman and when the task was labeled feminine.

The Makosky experiment is an important one, because it shows a link between the measured fear of success and subsequent behavior. [20] It also shows, however, that women who score high on fear of success are not afraid to compete in every situation—just in ones where the task is thought to be a masculine one or where competition is against a man. In these situations, we can assume that high-fear-of-success women anticipate that there will be negative consequences if they do succeed. In line with Horner's original suggestions, these women may fear that they will be rejected socially or that they will be considered unfeminine. Given no other information, these fears may be reasonable. But what if the situation is defined in such a way that these fears are not reasonable? Two recent studies have provided a fascinating look at what happens when the consequences are specified.

Social psychologist Jerald Jellison and his students made the rather simple suggestion that people will try to obtain positive consequences. [21] In any situation, a person's performance may be high or low depending on what will yield the best payoff. To test these straightforward assumptions, Jellison and his colleagues asked male and female college students to work on a set of intelligence tests. The students were told that a psychologist would be forming an impression of them based on their performance. Before beginning the test, the student was given a brief description of the psychologist's attitudes and values so that he or she would have some idea about the person who would be doing the evaluation. One of two different descriptions was given. One description indicated that the psychologist valued intelligence very highly, while the other description stated that the psychologist felt intelligence was generally a rather unimpressive characteristic in a person, far less important than many other traits.

The results of this study were as straightforward as the predictions. When people thought that the psychologist valued intelligence, they showed an increase in the level of their performance. When students thought that the psychologist was negative about intelligence, they showed a decrease in their performance. These results were true for both male and female students and were unaffected by the sex of the evaluating psychologist. Furthermore, it didn't matter whether the student was high or low on a fear-of-success measure: the performance was almost solely determined by the values of the evaluator.[22] People behaved in a way that would ensure themselves the most favorable consequences.

In a similar study done at Tulane University, women students were placed in a competitive situation with a male partner and, through the devices of the experimenters, either succeeded or failed in the competition.[23] After this competition, the woman "accidentally" heard her partner giving his impressions of her to the experimenter. These impressions were either favorable or unfavorable. Then the subject was asked to work on another task with a different partner. In this way the change in the subject's performance could be measured. Once again, the results showed that consequences make the difference. If the woman had been praised by her partner when she did poorly, she did worse on the second test. If she had been praised for doing well, her performance improved on the second test. Just the reverse happened when the subject had received a negative evaluation. She improved when she had been criticized for a negative performance, and she got worse when she had been criticized for a good performance.[24]

The conclusions that can be drawn from these two studies are quite clear. People (both men and women) will avoid success if the consequences of that success promise to be unpleasant. On the other hand, people will also avoid failure when that outcome promises to hold a negative payoff. After all, people are quite reasonable about their behavior much of the time, and most of us would rather have good things happen to us than bad things. I think it is safe to say that neither women nor men fear success per se, and when the consequences of success are made explicit, people will seek the good consequences and avoid the bad.

Yet these studies do not tell us what happens when the consequences are not clearly understood. In a more ambiguous situation, when the person does not know what the results will be, that person probably just has to guess at the consequences. And in this case, early socialization and/or recent experience will probably have an influence. If women have had more experiences with being criticized than being praised for doing well in a masculine situation, then they may indeed choose to avoid a successful performance. Or if men have been mocked for doing well in "girls' games," they too will probably seek to avoid appearing successful in similar situations. In neither case, however, would we be safe in assuming that the person was generally afraid of success—any success, all successes, or success in all situations. Fear of success is a relative thing.

Having traveled this far on the trail of achievement behavior, what can we conclude? While earlier investigators suggested that achievement motivation is primarily a male phenomenon, more recent research suggests that both men and women may strive to excel. The areas of striving may differ, and the consequences may vary as well. Yet the basic behaviors of men and women don't seem that different. For psychologists interested in the development of achievement theory, the task will be to relate the male-dominated traditional achievement theory with the female-dominated fear-of-success literature. Such an effort would surely help us understand the achievement behavior of humans.

Chapter 6

Communication Styles

*The world is the book of women. Whatever knowledge
they may possess is more commonly acquired by
observation than by reading.*

Rousseau

*If others know how you really feel, you can be hurt,
and that in itself is incompatible with manhood.*

Marc Feigen Fasteau

Much of our life involves communicating with other people.
Whether we are ordering a meal in a restaurant, shopping at the local
department store, or having a philosophical discussion with friends,
we are involved in the communication process. And when love or
friendship goes awry, people often claim a "breakdown in communication" as the cause.

For the human species, verbal language is the most obvious
form of communication. Virtually every interchange we have relies
on some form of the spoken or written word. Yet there are many
other ways that humans "speak" to each other. An old ballad
requests a lover to "drink to me only with thine eyes." The eyes can
indeed be a channel of communication; so can the expressions in a
face, the orientation of a body, and the touch of a hand.

It is particularly fascinating to consider the verbal and nonverbal patterns of communication used by men and women, in part
because the differences are so numerous. While researchers in many
areas have shied away from consideration of sex differences, students
of nonverbal communication have not been able to avoid the
question. Differences between men and women are pervasive in every
area of communication.

THE USES OF LANGUAGE

Let's begin with the most obvious form of communication—
verbal speaking behavior. Recall that in Chapter 1 we noted that
verbal ability is one of the few consistently established differences
between men and women. Although these differences are most

apparent after the age of 10 or 11, some investigations have shown that girls are more vocal than boys even in infancy.[1] By young adulthood, the differences are firmly established. On college entrance examinations, for example, verbal-aptitude scores for women are consistently higher than those of men.

Given women's greater verbal skills, we might expect to find that women are more proficient in their use of everyday language. In some instances, this is true. Studies have shown, for example, that women are more "correct" in their grammar, where correctness is determined by standard speech norms. Women are more likely to pronounce correctly a word like "dancing," while men are apt to slur the word into "dancin'."[2]

Other language differences between men and women do not relate directly to verbal ability. Perhaps the most pronounced difference between the sexes occurs in intonation patterns[3] or, in other words, the way phrases or sentences sound and vary in pitch. Some patterns seem to be exclusively feminine. For example, what has been labeled a "polite, cheerful pattern" consists of a definite upswing in pitch at the end of a sentence or request. Thus, in asking "Are you coming?" women would end the phrase at a much higher pitch, relative to where the sentence began, than would men.[4] Try saying this phrase a number of times, using different tonal patterns. Perhaps you can begin to spot the differences in the speech of those around you.

Some linguists have suggested other ways in which the speech patterns of men and women differ. Robin Lakoff believes that women are more likely to use tag-questions when they speak.[5] For example, a woman might say "This party is fun, isn't it?" but the man would be more likely to state "This party is fun." Yet while a number of people believe that this difference exists, there is little supporting evidence. This belief reflects a general tendency that prevails in the discussion of sex differences in language: people have many stereotypes about how men and women talk.

To demonstrate these stereotypes, Cheris Kramer collected a series of cartoons from the *New Yorker* magazine and analyzed them in terms of the sex of the speaker and the type of statement.[6] A number of strong differences appeared. In these cartoons, men spoke more often and spoke on more different topics. Men also spoke more forcefully and swore more often.* Women, in contrast, were pictured

*More than 50 years ago, a linguist named Otto Jesperson explained that women feel an "instinctive shrinking from coarse and gross expressions." Yet when presented with this observation, a number of modern women have been heard to reply "Oh, shit."

as qualifying their statements and showing more concern for the feelings and ideas of the person spoken to. Certain adjectives also were linked primarily to women. Few men, for example, said things were "cute" or "nice" or "pretty."

How many of these beliefs reflect the actual conversational patterns of men and women? To answer these questions, psychologists and linguists have been quite ingenious, using methods ranging from eavesdropping to telemetry. In one investigation, the authors "wore rubber heels and cultivated an unobtrusive manner" as they eavesdropped on people in the stores and on the streets of Columbus, Ohio.[7] In another study, a husband and wife agreed to wear miniature radio transmitters for the duration of a 16-hour day.[8] In yet another case, a mock jury was formed, using adults drawn from the regular jury pools of Chicago and St. Louis courts.[9] The most frequently observed sex difference in studies such as these is the amount of speech. In talking time, women are a clear second to men. Men also tend to initiate topics, while women are more likely to react to the comments of others. Other studies have shown that men are more likely to interrupt the speech of another. Women are less likely to interrupt a conversation, and when they themselves are interrupted, women generally don't attempt to recover the conversational lead.[10]

Less is known about content differences in the conversations of men and women. A number of early studies (done in the 1920s) found that women were most likely to talk about men and other women, whereas men more frequently discussed business and sports.[11] More recently, Elinor Langer found that women who work in the telephone company continue to avoid politics and religion in their conversations, but the telephone company men often centered discussions around politics.[12] The difficulty with these studies is that they are either quite dated (prior to the original women's suffrage movement) or confounded by other factors such as occupational status. I would be willing to bet that if someone were to compare the conversations of men and women today in similar job settings, the topical differences would be very slight.

At a more personal level of conversation, clearer differences between men and women have been shown. A number of laboratory studies have been conducted in which people are asked to reveal personal information about themselves to both friends and strangers. The majority of these studies show that women are much more willing to disclose information about themselves than are men.[13] (While a few studies show no differences between the sexes, none has pointed to greater disclosure by men.)[14] Men, in fact, cast a somewhat jaundiced eye at other men who are willing to discuss personal information.[15] Men like other men who disclose relatively little information about themselves, whereas women consistently show a preference for those women who are willing to discuss personal information.

Writers such as Marc Fasteau have also commented on the unwillingness of men to disclose their fears to other men, pointing to the disadvantages of self-disclosure in a competitive relationship.[16] The late Sidney Jourard, in discussing these differences between men and women, suggested that the male role was a "lethal" one.[17] Because men do not readily express their fears and doubts, Jourard felt men are adding stresses that cause a shorter life span. Unfortunately, we know little about the relationship between self-disclosure and longevity and relatively little about self-disclosure outside the laboratory environment. Furthermore, few studies of self-disclosure have considered opposite-sex pairs. The interactions between men and women may be important areas of self-disclosure that deserve additional study.[18]

So far we have looked only at the verbal means of communicating. Yet as mentioned earlier, people are able to communicate vast amounts of information through nonverbal channels: the knowing glance, the meaningful touch, and the declarative gesture. In the discussion that follows, we'll consider sex differences in these nonverbal forms of communication.

THE VISUAL WORLD

The human species has a well-developed sense of vision, and it is logical that this visual sense would be used as a means of receiving and sending information. Social psychologist Ralph Exline and his collaborators have extensively studied the use of eye contact in dyadic communication.[19] In a typical situation, two people are asked to talk to one another while the investigators record the amount of eye contact. In nearly every instance, women spend more time looking directly at the other person than do men. Not only do women make more eye contact than men, but they also seem to rely more heavily on this form of communication. In one study, Michael Argyle asked subjects to talk to each other, but in some cases a barrier was placed between the two people so that they could not see each other.[20] Women reported that they were much more uncomfortable in this situation, and they talked less than when they were able to see their partner. Men, on the other hand, were more talkative when they could not see their partner and did not seem to feel any discomfort when they were separated by a partition.

What do the eyes see? Is there a function being served in eye contact? It seems reasonable to assume that, if you are looking directly at another individual, you will be more aware of his or her facial expressions and perhaps bodily cues as well. Students of nonverbal communication have shown us that there are many channels of communication beyond speech, and the research suggests that women use these channels more often than men. Are women any better at interpreting this kind of information? The available evidence indicates that they are.

In one study of this problem, Ross Buck and his colleagues considered how emotions are communicated through facial expressions.[21] Subjects were tested in pairs, either both females or both males. One subject, who was called the "sender," was seated in front of a projection screen on which color slides were presented. These slides were divided into five categories: sexual, scenic, maternal, disgusting, and ambiguous. As the "sender" was looking at the slide, the other subject, called the "observer," was watching the facial expressions of the "sender." The task for the observer was to read the expression of the sender and try to determine what the sender's emotional reactions to the slide were. The observer was asked to judge which of five categories of slides was being shown to the sender and how pleasant and intense the sender's emotional reaction was. In this competition between the sexes, women won hands down. In nine of the ten female pairs, the observer was able to identify the slide category at better than a chance percentage, whereas only three of the nine male pairs showed as good a batting average.

Although this experiment rather clearly shows females to be better at the task, some questions remain. Because members of each pair were of the same sex, it is difficult to tell where the superiority lies. Were women senders able to communicate emotion more effectively than male senders? Or were women observers better able to read the expressions of their senders? Either or both of these statements may be true.

Buck and his colleagues had these same questions, and they conducted a second study to provide some answers.[22] With all possible combinations of males and females as senders and observers, this second study showed that the major sex difference occurred among the senders. Women were considerably more effective in communicating their emotional responses to the pictures than were men, while men and women did not differ in their accuracy as observers.

Yet while women apparently *can* convey their emotions more clearly, it is not necessarily true that they always do. Interestingly enough, both men and women feel the opposite sex is more expressive in depicting their emotions.[23] Though little research has been done, I suspect that this general belief would depend on the particular emotion in question. For example, which sex do you think would express sadness more clearly? Which sex would express more anger?

Many people have observed that women smile more often than men. As a simple test of this trend, go through your high school yearbook. Look at how many men versus women are giving wide open grins, how many have closed-lip smiles, and how many are looking rather stern. When I did this simple survey, the findings were clear. Women are much more likely to show wide grins, and men are more apt to adopt a stern no-nonsense pose. As for the compromise, smiling but not committing your teeth to the effort, men also choose this tactic more than females. Given that this is a situation in which people are usually encouraged to "smile at the camera," the existence of such a pronounced difference seems particularly telling.

Current feminist analyses point to the smile as the equivalent of the Uncle Tom shuffle—a gesture made to indicate submissiveness in the face of a superior. In animal literature, there is evidence that at least monkeys use the smile in this way. In her fascinating study of the chimpanzees of the Gombe Stream in Tanzania, Jane Van Lawick-Goodall observed animals smiling when they wished to avoid conflict with a higher-status compatriot.[24] Can we say that women smile for the same reasons, to affirm their inferior status? I'll allow you to reach your own conclusions.

The fact that women do smile more, however, leads to some very interesting consequences. Daphne Bugental and her colleagues have conducted a fascinating series of studies dealing with the relationship of facial expressions to verbal messages.[25] In studying the behavior of parents with their children, these psychologists found that fathers tended to smile when they were saying positive things, and not to smile when they were not saying positive things. That seems a reasonable state of affairs. Yet the verbal messages of mothers were not more likely to be positive when they were smiling than when they weren't. In other words, these "perfidious feminine faces" could smile when they were making negative remarks or frown when they were saying positive things. In a further study, Bugental and her colleagues asked children to interpret situations in which either a woman or a man was conveying one message with his or her face while conveying a contradictory message verbally. In judging women, children tended to believe the verbal message and ignore the smile. With men, children believed that the smile indicated friendliness and relied more on its message. One interpretation of these findings is that because women smile so often the message of the smile is unclear. A cue that is present all the time, in a variety of different situations, does not tell us much about different states of mind.

We have seen that women can be better "senders" of emotion on some occasions, when the message is not overlaid with a ubiquitous smile. But what of women as receivers? In the study by Buck and his colleagues in which observers had to categorize facial expressions into five different groups, no differences between men and women were found. Yet a more elaborate series of studies by Robert Rosenthal and his colleagues have found consistent sex differences. [26] In these studies, subjects are asked to interpret 11 different patterns of nonverbal behavior, combining facial expressions, body positions, and vocal patterns. With these more complex stimuli, women consistently perform better than men. An interesting exception to this general pattern of female superiority is a group of men in occupations such as acting, art, and mental health. Men in these groups are generally equal to or better than women in reading nonverbal cues.

Women's greater skills in reading nonverbal cues may be related to their tendency to make more eye contact. For ages, women's intuition has been a source of either amazement or ridicule, but it may be based on some very objective data. If the woman is using more of the nonverbal channels of communication to collect information, she may have a broader, or at least a different, base on which to make predictions about the behavior of other people. While the man is engaged in more verbal interchange, the woman may be collecting information in these other categories. Thus, the "intuitive" conclusion, which frequently seems to contradict the apparent verbal information, may in fact be an equally objective judgment—just one based on different information.

THE TOUCH

Touching is another way to communicate with people, expressing a range of emotions from the hostile punch to the loving stroke. Once again, this mode of communication reveals sex differences. Men are more likely to touch others, and women are more likely to be touched. [27] The reactions of women and men to being touched can differ also. In one ingenious investigation of these reactions, Jeffrey Fisher, Marvin Rytting, and Richard Heslin looked at the effects of being touched in an accidental way. [28] Gaining the cooperation of library personnel, these investigators arranged to have library clerks (both male and female) either touch or not touch the hands of students who were checking out books. The touch in this case was a very brief one, making contact with the student's hand for about one-half second as the student's ID card was being returned. Soon after each student left the check-out desk, he or she was approached by an experimenter with a questionnaire concerning the library and its personnel. Although this questionnaire was not specifically related to the student's previous experience with the clerk, the effects of that experience were nonetheless evident. Women who had been briefly touched by the clerk reported feeling generally more positive than women who had not and reacted more favorably toward both the clerk and the library setting. For men, in contrast, the touch seemed to have little effect on their feelings. The sex of the library clerk had no influence on these results, perhaps because of the relative neutrality of the interchange. It is particularly interesting to note that many of the subjects in this study reported that they were not aware they had been touched by the clerk. Yet despite their nonawareness, these students indicated the same positive feelings or negative feelings as did students who were aware of the casual touch.

Why do women respond more positively to being touched? To explore one possible reason, we should note that sex differences in touching behavior tend to parallel status differences.[29] Between persons of different ranks, the dominant one will do more of the touching and the subordinate one will be touched more often. Thus, if we consider that at least some forms of touch convey status messages, it is not surprising that the typically dominant male would initiate touching, while the more subordinate female would be the recipient. As an example of this difference, consider how often a boy puts his arm around a girl. Now consider what happens if a girl puts her arm around a boy, initiating the contact. Frequently, observers will tend to view that girl as being overly aggressive or as making inappropriate sexual moves.

Women may also have more experience with being touched, because same-sex touching is more allowable for females. Apart from the formal handshake, males rarely touch other males, and even a brush may be interpreted as a homosexual advance. Perhaps the major exception occurs when men are together in a situation in which physical contact is legitimized. In a football game, for example, every fan is familiar with the backpatting among players that is so rarely seen elsewhere. The traditionally masculine image of these sports may dispel negative connotations that occur in more ordinary situations.

DIMENSIONS OF PERSONAL SPACE

Possibly reflecting their more positive feelings about physical contact, women are more comfortable being close to people than are men. Many studies of what social scientists call "distancing behavior" show that American men prefer greater distances between themselves and another person than do women. This behavior has been observed in many settings. Women stand closer to other women than men do to other men in public exhibits.[30] They sit closer when they are in an experimental laboratory.[31] They will walk up closer to another woman whose eyes are shut than will men to a male partner.[32]

In addition to these distance patterns, there are directional differences between men and women as well. For example, one study has reported that women are more likely to approach strangers from the front, while men are more likely to make an approach from the side.[33] These patterns of preference for the front versus the side have also been observed in a college library setting.[34] When men sit alone at a table, they are most likely to pile their books in front of them, providing a barrier to a frontal approach. Women, in contrast, tend to pile their books to the side. Similarly, both sexes tend to report negative feelings when they are approached from the less preferred direction—men from the front and women from the side. It would be interesting to learn how general this pattern is. Do men and women position themselves differently in airport lounges, doctors' waiting rooms, and cocktail parties? The previous research suggests that such differences would be found. The reasons for this difference are less clear. Perhaps because women make more use of eye contact, a frontal approach is preferred. Other writers have suggested that men dislike the face-to-face approach because it implies some form of dominance threat. Whatever the reasons, men and women have once again shown themselves to behave differently.

How can we explain all of these differences? In nearly every area we have considered, women are more likely to prefer reduced distances and greater contact, while men prefer greater distances and less contact. Perhaps these patterns relate to differences between the sexes in the need for power and affiliation. Affiliation basically means getting closer to other people, both physically and psychologically, and most measures have shown that women express more positive feelings about social interactions.[35] The nonverbal behaviors of getting close, making more eye contact, and being touched would all contribute to these affiliative motives. Self-disclosure can also create feelings of friendship and intimacy. Men, on the other hand, express relatively weaker affiliation needs but are stronger than women in their expressed needs for dominance. Exerting power and control can be accomplished in a number of ways, such as interrupting conversations and talking at greater length. As we've seen, some forms of touching can also serve as a demonstration of this kind of control. Yet many other forms of nonverbal contact, such as distancing and being touched, must be regulated if power is to be exercised. Getting too close may imply a lack of control, just as disclosing information about oneself makes one potentially more vulnerable.

In fact, those factors necessary to maintain a sense of control are almost the mirror opposite of those factors that increase affiliation. Men and women seem to have opted for opposite sides of the mirror, and their communication styles reflect these choices in a clear and readable way.

Chapter 7

Altruism: Helping and Being Helped

*The weakness of their reasoning faculty also explains
why women show more sympathy for the unfortunate
than men. . . .*

Schopenhauer

From the chivalry codes of the Middle Ages to more recent-vintage etiquette books, men have been encouraged to protect the woman from a variety of discomforts and misfortunes. In earlier periods, men laid down their coats to protect the feet of the woman who encountered a puddle and walked on the outside of the street to offer protection against garbage thrown from overhanging windows.[1] In more recent times, tossing one's coat casually into a puddle has not been demanded, but etiquette books still recommend that men walk on the outside of the street, open doors, light cigarettes, and act as the general protector in situations requiring action. Given this history of instruction, it is perhaps no surprise to find that men are indeed more likely to offer help and women are more likely to receive help.

MAY I BE OF SOME ASSISTANCE?

Social psychologists have documented many instances in which people may offer their help to a person in trouble. The trouble may be minor, falling very much within the territory of etiquette-book prescriptions. For example, Bibb Latané and James Dabbs, Jr., arranged for some of their students to walk around dropping pencils or coins in elevators.[2] The students then kept track of who offered to help them pick up the fallen objects, an act considered to be a form of altruism, or helping behavior. As prescribed by etiquette (and predicted by social psychologists as well), men were much more likely to volunteer their services than were women. At the same time, the female pencil-dropper received considerably more assistance from fellow passengers than did the equally clumsy male. Geography appears to affect chivalry, however. This same field experiment was conducted in Atlanta, in Seattle, and in Columbus, Ohio, and the percentages of people offering help showed striking differences in the different locations. When a woman dropped pencils in Atlanta, Georgia, for example, nearly 70% of the male bystanders offered help, while only 32% of the males in Columbus were inclined to be so helpful. These differences work in the other direction as well. Men who dropped pencils in Atlanta were helped only 10% of the time when a woman was present, while the women of Columbus offered help on 25% of the occasions. Thus, although chivalry appears to be alive and well in the South, it is clearly experiencing some illness in the Midwest. (In both instances, the behavior of Seattle citizens fell midway between the behaviors observed in the other two cities.)

Other situations in which another person appears to need help may involve much more effort. What if, for example, you are sitting on a bus or subway and a man falls down in front of you, apparently suffering from some illness? Or to make it worse, what if the man is obviously drunk? In this case, a person who wanted to help would have to go over to the fallen body, attempt to discover the problem, and possibly assist the person to a seat. As the effort and in some cases the physical strength that are required increase, it becomes increasingly likely that more men than women will choose to intervene and offer their help. In a study using this body-in-the-subway situation, for instance, it was found that nearly 90% of those persons who tried to help were males.[3]

Other situations in which greater effort is required of the potential helper include the frequently observed case of the flat tire on the highway. In their original study of this situation, psychologists James Bryan and Mary Ann Test arranged for a female confederate to be parked at the side of a highway, apparently in need of help with her car.[4] Nearly everyone who offered help was a man. An attractive woman does better in this situation than an unattractive one. When investigators have compared the frequency of help offered to a woman who is dressed in an unattractive fashion (baggy sweatshirt and long loose skirt) as compared to an attractively dressed "lady in distress" (in shorts and a midriff top), it is clear that the more attractive woman fares better.[5]

Neither of these "flat tire" studies included conditions in which a man needed help, however, so from these studies we can't yet conclude that women are more likely to receive help in these situations than are men. Perhaps both sexes will receive an equal amount of help when the need is great. However, in a study by Richard Pomazal and Gerald Clore, both males and females were used as victims of the flat tire.[6] Their findings are quite clear: if you're a man, don't expect many people to offer to help you change a flat tire. In 200 cases where a man had a flat tire, only four people offered to help (a 2% rate of helping). The woman, in contrast, received help approximately 25% of the time. As in the previous study, nearly all of the people who offered to help the motorist were men: only two out of 53 persons who stopped to help were women. Of course, it is possible that many women don't know how to change a tire. Perhaps they would be more willing to help if the distressed motorist appeared to want a ride to the nearest gas station rather than direct physical help with the tire. To test this possibility, Pomazal and Clore arranged for a male or female to be standing next to a car at the side of a highway and to make standard hitchhiking signs, indicating that they wanted a ride. While help in this situation would presumably require less knowledge and less effort on the part of the helper, the basic findings did not change. Women were still much more likely to receive help, and men were the principal offerers of help.

WOMEN, MEN, AND INTERVENTION

In each of the situations that we have discussed so far, the request for help is indirect at best. A bystander witnesses an event in which it seems likely that another person could use some help. The observer then has to decide whether he or she will intervene in the situation and offer assistance. In these intervention situations, two patterns are clear: women receive more help than men, and men offer more help than women. Why do these persistent differences between men and women occur?

The fact that women are helped more than men (in other words, the difference between men and women as a stimulus characteristic) may be a direct consequence of the stereotypes that are held in our society. As we saw in Chapter 2, women as a group are characterized as less competent, less capable of making decisions, and more excitable in minor crises. Given these assumptions, it seems logical that the woman would be perceived as having a greater need for help. Men, on the other hand, are assumed to be independent, strong, competent, and self-reliant. With all of these things going for them, why do they need help? These stereotypes may explain why women receive more help when an observer must decide whether help is needed. But why do men give more help? There are at least three possible explanations for this difference.

One possibility is that the intervention studies have dealt with situations that women may be less adept at handling. Changing a tire, for example, has traditionally been considered a masculine activity, and perhaps women feel less capable of being helpful in this situation. What would happen if the situation were one in which women could be assumed to be more knowledgeable? For example, if a small child were crying in a department store, apparently having lost its parents, would men or women be more likely to help? It is possible that we would find a reversal in this situation. On the other hand, many of the helping studies discussed have not been so clearly sex-linked in their requirements. It is difficult to argue that men are more knowledgeable in picking up pencils or in driving a stranded motorist to a gas station. Thus, while some studies may reflect differences in task familiarity, this explanation does not cover enough of the data.

A second possibility is that the rewards and costs involved in helping are different for women and men. Picking up a hitchhiker, for example, can sometimes lead to disastrous consequences. Newspapers frequently report stories of robberies and rapes befalling the charitable driver. These potential costs may be greater for the woman than for the man, in that she typically has less strength to counter an aggressive hitchhiker. Similarly, the woman in the subway may be more vulnerable to the drunken passenger who has fallen down or may have less physical strength to enable her to pick him up. The rewards in helping situations may differ for men and women as well. If our stereotypes stipulate that men are supposed to be the protectors and women the protected, then perhaps the payoffs for these behaviors correspond. A man who offers help may be fulfilling his role expectations and may receive praise accordingly. In contrast, if a woman offers help, particularly to a man, the response may be one of thanks mixed with embarrassment. An illustration of this ambivalence was shown by one of my students who observed women opening doors for men. Although some men seemed quite pleased, others reacted with embarrassment and still others indicated suspicion and ridicule. Thus, the woman who offers help may receive fewer rewards than the comparable man. Balancing these costs and rewards, helping behavior may be more profitable for men than for women.

A third explanation for the observed sex differences is that men are simply more likely to intervene in any situation. If men have been trained to be the initiators, whereas women feel more comfortable in reacting to the initiations of others (a pattern observed in conversational styles), then it would make sense that men would be the ones to offer help when no direct request had been made. The more intervention required, the more often we would expect to see men exceeding women in offers of help. In support of this argument, those few studies that have found no differences between the helping behavior of men and women have generally involved reporting rather than doing. For example, Richard Page and Martin Moss found that, when a pedestrian dropped a package on the street, men and women did not differ in their overall tendency to help. However, men were more likely to pick up the package, while women tended to simply notify the pedestrian of the loss.[7] In another case, where "intervention" simply called for a person to pick up an envelope lying on the ground and put the envelope in a mailbox, men again showed no greater helping behavior than women.[8] Thus, the more assertive the potential helper has to be, the more likely men are to be the helpers.

DIRECT REQUESTS FOR HELP

So far, we have considered only situations in which the helper must decide for himself or herself whether help is needed and then make a decision about intervening in the situation. Yet in life there are many occasions in which we are directly asked for assistance. A volunteer comes to the door collecting for the Heart Fund. A stranger stops you on the street and asks for directions to the nearest restaurant. Someone calls you on the phone and asks for your support of Candidate Jones. In each of these situations, the other person makes it clear that help is needed, and our only decision is whether or not to agree with their request.

What might we expect to happen in these direct request situations, based on our previous discussion of intervention helping? First of all, sex of the person receiving help should be less important. We have hypothesized that people offer more help to women because of a stereotyped belief that the woman has a greater need for help. But if the person, either a man or a woman, directly asks for our help, then we don't have to rely on these assumptions. The person has told us that she or he needs help.

Social scientists have conducted numerous studies in which one person asks another for help, and in most of these studies the sex of the person asking for help has made no difference. The one major exception was found when the person requesting help stressed his or her dependency on the potential helper. In this study by Charles Gruder and Thomas Cook, subjects who reported for a psychology experiment found that the experimenter was absent but that a note had been left for the subject to read.[9] The note explained that the experimenter (who was either a male or a female, as designated by the signature on the note and by personal belongings lying about the room) had been called away but asked that the subject assist the experimenter during the scheduled experimental time. Help in this instance consisted of stapling some questionnaires that were needed by the experimenter. In the high-dependency condition, subjects were told that the experimenter needed the questionnaires within two hours, while, in a low-dependency condition, the questionnaires were not needed for a week. The number of questionnaires subjects assembled was used as a measure of helping behavior. Did the sex of the unseen experimenter make a difference in this case? When the experimenter's need was not great, there was no real difference. However, when the experimenter expressed a strong need, both men and women subjects were more willing to offer help to the female experimenter. In this case, a statement of high need by a woman may carry more weight than a similar statement by a man. In the less pressing situation, and in most other request situations, however, men and women receive help in about the same proportions.

If sex of the person being helped is less important in request situations, what happens with sex as a subject variable? Do men continue to show more willingness to help in these situations? Overall, the answer is no. There is no general tendency for men to be more helpful in these situations. To understand why this equality is so, let's again look back to our previous points of discussion. We considered three possible reasons for the greater willingness of men to offer help. One related to the act of intervention itself, which is not applicable in the present request situations. The other two possibilities concerned the nature of the task and differences in rewards and costs experienced by men and women. Both of these factors appear to play a more important role in situations where help is directly requested.

Many requests for help are quite neutral with regard to sex-linkage. For example, requests for a donation to the Cancer Fund or a dime for a phone call appear to have little masculine or feminine characteristics involved. In these situations, our explanation that relies on task characteristics should not predict differences between men and women in their willingness to help. And indeed, few sex differences are found in these situations. One study that did find a difference involved making a phone call. Individuals were called at home, presumably by someone who had dialed a wrong number in an attempt to reach Ralph's Garage. The caller explained that he had used his last dime and asked the "subject" to call the garage and explain the situation to Ralph. Men were far more willing than women to make this call.[10] Possibly these results reflect the fact that men are generally more familiar with garages and have had more experience with mechanics. If the request had been to call a nursery school, would women have been more likely to agree to help?

To test this connection between the type of task and the sex of the helper, some psychologists at the University of Illinois set up the following field experiment.[11] Shoppers in a local drugstore were approached by either a young man or a young woman who explained that he or she was in a real hurry and had to go next door on another errand. The young man or woman then asked the shopper to do a favor by buying one item and provided the shopper with a dollar bill to make the purchase. One of two items was requested by the experimenter: either chewing tobacco or a depilatory. Although the sex of the experimenter had no effect in this study, the type of item did. Male shoppers were more likely to agree to make the purchase of chewing tobacco, while women showed more help when a depilatory was to be purchased. Apparently, the type of request does make a difference in direct request situations. Both sexes are more likely to agree to help when the task is appropriate for their sex.

Our third explanation for sex differences in helping behavior points to different costs and rewards in the helping situation. Few of the direct request situations have looked at instances where costs are terribly high, and almost never is there any physical harm or danger involved. Thus, the kinds of costs that might have caused a difference when picking up a hitchhiker are not really a factor in the request situations that have been investigated. However, the reward question does seem to be important, particularly when we consider various combinations of males and females in the request situation.

THE REWARDS OF THE OPPOSITE SEX

Leonard Bickman conducted a series of studies in which students asked other students to volunteer their help for a psychology experiment.[12] In two of these studies, male or female experimenters called both male and female students and asked if they could spend anywhere from two to eight hours participating in a perception experiment. Both of these studies showed a clear cross-sex effect: males were more likely to volunteer when they were called by a female, and females were more likely to agree when a male voice was at the other end of the phone. Bickman found the same effect when students received a letter from either a male or female student who needed help with the psychology experiment. In this case, even though no direct contact was involved, students were more likely to agree to help an opposite-sexed classmate.

Why are we more likely to help someone of the opposite sex?

While it is possible to think of a number of reasons, perhaps the best explanation is that interaction with the opposite sex promises to be a more rewarding experience for many people. Other research has shown that both men and women find positive evaluations from the opposite sex to be more rewarding than identical evaluations from the same sex.[13] In a similar fashion, an anticipated "thank you" or other forms of possible gratitude from the recipient of your help may be a more powerful enticement when it is connected with an opposite-sex person. Although some people have argued that cross-sex helping is more frequent because the helper is anticipating some larger future payoff for being nice, such as a date or a romance, this explanation seems needlessly overburdened. In fact, Bickman showed in one of his studies that students were just as likely to agree with the request of an opposite-sex caller when the actual future contact would be with a same-sex student. These findings would suggest that the immediate reinforcement or experience is more important than any long-term goals of ingratiating oneself with the person requesting help.

At least this explanation seems to be true when the potential helper is contacted by telephone or by letter. We might expect that the same kinds of things would happen when the request was more direct, such as when someone walks up to you and asks if you can help. Somewhat surprisingly, the results of several studies suggest that this is a different situation. Cross-sex effects are not nearly as common in these face-to-face situations. For example, using the same dialogue in a direct encounter asking for help in a psychology experiment, Bickman found that sex had no effect. There were no differences between men and women in their willingness to help or in the likelihood of being helped, and the previously found cross-sex effect did not appear. Similarly, Latané and Darley found no cross-sex effects when an experimenter asked pedestrians for 20¢.[14] In contrast to these studies of face-to-face interaction that found no cross-sex effects, a number of other studies do show evidence of opposite-sex preference. In one such study, persons wearing hearing aids approached individuals in Grand Central Station and, by means of a written note, asked the individual to make a phone call.[15] Under these conditions, there was evidence that men were more likely to help women and women were more likely to help men. In a similar study, students at Purdue University were approached by a stranger and asked if they could lend the stranger a dime for a phone call.[16] Once again, there was a strong tendency for cross-sex helping to be more frequent.

These results don't seem to give us a very clear picture about what happens when requests for help are given in a face-to-face setting. Perhaps part of the answer lies in the fact that a face-to-face interaction provides many different kinds of cues besides sex. The race of the person, the kind of clothes being worn, how attractive the person is, the style of speaking—each of these may affect how willing someone is to help the person asking for help. Actually, some of the studies discussed above were primarily focusing on variables other than sex, such as race and style of clothing, and the results showed that these other factors have an important influence on helping behavior.

When we have only minimal information about someone of the opposite sex, such as a voice or a name, we may be free to form our own images. In our fantasy life, these imaginary people may fit our ideal man or woman. They may dress a certain way, be highly attractive, and have a whole set of traits we personally like. And when this nearly anonymous person asks for help, we may be quite ready to offer our assistance. In contrast to these fantasies, actual interactions with other men and women may present us with a number of characteristics we don't like. Women may like men and men may like women in general terms, but a particular Jane or Joe may be not at all likable. While this additional information may not totally eliminate the cross-sex helping effect, the available evidence suggests a substantially weakened preference for helping the opposite sex when the additional information is available.

In statistical terms, I am suggesting that there is more variability in the face-to-face situation. In less formal terms, many other factors besides sex may play a role, and because people vary widely in the characteristics they like and dislike, single-minded preferences for the opposite sex may not appear as clearly. But what would happen if we were able to establish the same kind of impression that each person had of the individual who was asking for help? Although this would be difficult to do in terms of physical characteristics,[17] it is less difficult to arrange in terms of behavior. For example, most people tend to like someone who is nice to them. Thus, if we could establish a situation in which we were fairly sure that each individual subject had a rather positive impression of the person who was asking for help, we could then see if cross-sex helping would again become more prominent. Michael Hendricks, Thomas Cook, and William Crano developed just this kind of situation.[18] Before considering their particular manipulations of liking, let's first look at their general scenario. In a library at Michigan State University, experimental confederates sat down at a table across from a student, who thereby became a subject in the experiment. The confederate, whom we shall call the victim, took off his or her watch and set it down between himself or herself and the subject. After a few minutes of studying, the victim left the table, leaving books and watch behind. Then came the thief. From the next table, another student walked over to the table where the subject was sitting, picked up the victim's watch, and then left the room. After the thief had made his getaway, the victim returned, noticed that the watch was missing, and urgently asked the subject if he or she knew what had happened to it. Helping behavior in this rather elaborately planned situation was the responsiveness of the subject to the victim's loss. Varying degrees of help were recorded: denying that anything had been seen, admitting having seen the theft but offering no help in identification, pointing out the thief (who by this time had returned to his seat at the next table), or directly intervening when the crime occurred. (Relatively few people intervened before the victim returned, and as we might have expected from the earlier discussion, interveners were most likely to be men and intervention was most likely to occur when the victim was a woman.)

Now for the manipulation of liking. Before the theft occurred, the victim had some contact with the subject. In a series of control conditions, this contact was rather neutral and was not expected to produce any particular feelings in the subject toward the victim. These conditions would be similar to some of the face-to-face interaction studies discussed earlier. In the main experimental condition, in contrast, the experimenters tried to establish some positive feeling for the victim. Their method of doing this was fairly simple—the victim offered the subject a stick of gum. While such an offer is not momentous, it is a friendly thing to do, and we can assume that most of the subjects liked the victim better in this condition than in the control conditions.

How did this favor affect the willingness of the subject to help the victim after the theft? The main result was that cross-sex helping increased substantially: men were much more likely to help the female victim, and women were much more likely to help the male victim. Same-sex helping, in contrast, showed a tendency to decrease under these conditions. Despite the fact that this experimental situation was both elaborate and unique, the results do point to some conditions when cross-sex helping will be most common in face-to-face interactions. When a person is free to make assumptions about how likable the other person is, or when liking is somehow established, cross-sex helping seems to be more common than same-sex helping. But if neither of these conditions is met, then other factors come into play and the cross-sex helping effect may be weakened.

The question of whether men or women are more helpful is

surely not a simple one. Schopenhauer's early belief of greater female sympathy has been translated into many forms, including a suggestion that there is a general norm of social responsibility that women adhere to more strongly. Yet the research is not so obliging. Sometimes women are more helpful, but on other occasions men are more helpful, and at still other times the sexes are equally altruistic in their behavior. One possible conclusion from these apparently contradictory findings is that there is no difference between men and women in willingness to give help. Our situational perspective allows another conclusion, however. Amidst the chaos, there are some clear patterns to male and female altruism. First, a distinction can be made between situations that require the helper to take the initiative and those in which the helper responds to a direct request. In the former case, men help more than women, perhaps because of a greater tendency to intervene rather than react. In request situations, we find that the sex differences are more variable. Now two other factors seem to play an important role: first, the extent to which the task is linked to traditionally masculine or feminine characteristics, and second, the rewards that the helper will receive. If all else is equal, rewards from the opposite sex seem to have a higher value. Armed with these explanations, we can find a pattern in the research on altruism. The behavior of women and men may be complex, but it is not beyond comprehension for those who are patient.

Chapter 8

Aggression

Woman is deprived of the lessons of violence by her
nature . . . her muscular weakness disposes her
to passivity.

Simone de Beauvoir

Becoming masculine does not involve simple "imprinting."
One has to dare certain activities which are dangerous
and can be painful. There is nothing automatic about
fighting.

Norman Mailer

Men are more aggressive than women. This statement of a consistent sex difference is one of the few generalizations that has held up under the analysis of cautious investigators. As we saw in Chapter 1, evidence from biology, socialization, and cross-cultural contexts supports the belief that men and women typically differ in this behavior.

Social psychologists studying aggression have translated this belief into practice. For example, during an 18-month period in 1971 and 1972, the major journals in social psychology published 24 articles dealing with aggression. Nineteen of these articles used only males as subjects. Four additional studies used both males and females (though only one of these checked to see if there were differences between the sexes), and one additional article did not mention what sex of subject was used.[1]

Despite these beliefs and practices, it is clear that women can be as aggressive as men on some occasions. One glance at the crime rates should dispel any doubts of the woman's ability in this regard. While the absolute numbers for men are greater, there have always been women who commit violent crimes. Furthermore, in the decade from 1960 to 1970, the number of women arrested for crimes increased 74% (compared to 25% for men), and the increase in violent crimes for women was nearly as high (69%). Surely biology has not altered in that short period, so we must conclude that women are either learning to be more aggressive or are becoming more willing to display aggressive behavior.

This distinction between learning and performance is an important one and may help us to understand some of the differences between women and men. Recall that when we discussed aggression in Chapter 1, we found some evidence for a biological component that may predispose men to be more aggressive. However, this biological factor, if it does exist, only creates a greater readiness to learn aggressive behavior. The individual, whether male or female, must still acquire the relevant behaviors and then choose to act in an aggressive manner. Some evidence suggests that women do quite well in the learning stage but simply hold back in the performance. Albert Bandura has demonstrated this point quite convincingly in an experiment with children.[2] He asked children to watch a filmed sequence of an adult hitting and kicking a large rubber Bobo doll. After this film was shown, children had an opportunity to play with the same Bobo doll, and Bandura observed the amount of aggressive behavior the children had presumably learned from the film. When simply given the opportunity to repeat the observed behavior, boys showed more aggression than did girls. However, in a second part of this same study, Bandura offered children rewards for performing as many of the model's behaviors as they could remember. With this new incentive, the girls became much more aggressive than they were previously, and few sex differences were apparent.

Apparently girls and women can learn to be as aggressive as boys and men. But what are the conditions that encourage women to show this ability for aggression? Let's look at the evidence.

MEN AND WOMEN AS AGGRESSORS

The tendency for researchers to use only men in studying aggression may have derived from one of two sources. First, investigators of aggressive behavior (nearly all men in the past) may have been reluctant to expose women to the electric shock typically used in laboratory studies of aggression. A second possibility is that investigators were influenced by the early findings, which typically showed men to be more aggressive than women.

An example of these early experiments on aggression is a study conducted by Arnold Buss.[3] Students who reported for a psychology experiment were told that they would be participating in a teacher and learner situation. Although two students showed up at the same time, only one was a real subject. The other student was a confederate of the experimenter. The real subject was assigned the role of the teacher, which involved administering shocks to the learner when an incorrect response was made on a memory task. Because the learner was actually a confederate of the experimenter, he or she could arrange to make a number of mistakes deliberately. The problem for the subject was to decide how much shock to give the learner for his or her errors. In this situation, male college students gave significantly higher levels of shock to the learner than did female subjects.

The greater willingness of men to act aggressively against a passive learner persists even when a third party is making the decisions about appropriate shock levels.[4] In this case, the teacher is told by an authority what shock he or she should give, and the levels of shock are increased as the experiment continues. Even though the decision is made by another person, women continue to show more reluctance to shock the learner.[5]

Stuart Taylor and Seymour Epstein also looked at the differences between male and female aggression in a laboratory setting.[6] However, in their study aggression was not a one-way street. Subjects were allowed to give shock to another student, but they could also receive shocks from that other person. Initially, the men in the Taylor and Epstein study showed substantially more aggression than did the women, as in the earlier study by Buss. But as the partner started becoming more aggressive, females responded in kind, and by the end of the session there was little difference between men and women in the amount of shock they were giving their partners.

Two other psychologists, Jack Hokanson and Robert Edelman, have also found that women will be just as aggressive as men when they are provoked by a shocking partner.[7] An intriguing finding of their study, however, is that the physiological reactions of men and women still differ despite the equivalence in behavior. Measuring increases and decreases in systolic blood pressure, these psychologists found that men show a quick recovery after making an aggressive response, while women do not recover as quickly. These authors suggest that past socialization pressures may allow men to feel relief after "solving" a situation by means of aggression, but for women aggression may create greater anxiety. In a later study, these same authors found that if women are allowed to make a friendly gesture in response to the aggression of their partner, they show faster physiological recovery than when they are aggressive.[8] For men, making a friendly response doesn't do the job. These results are intriguing. They suggest that while both men and women may be able to act aggressively when the situation calls for it, men find this kind of behavior less disturbing. The behavior may be similar, but the reactions of the man and woman to their own behavior may differ, possibly as a result of early training.[9]

Before considering these differences further, let's look at some studies of aggression that have been conducted outside the confines of the laboratory. Probably most of you have had the experience of being in a car, coming to a stop at a red traffic light, and then not immediately noticing when the light turns green. Particularly those of you who live in a fast-paced urban center such as New York City may also have experienced a loud honk from the driver behind you, who obviously noticed the light change before you did. Social psychologists Anthony Doob and Alan Gross have interpreted this behavior as a form of aggression, and they considered whether men were more likely to be aggressive in this situation than were women. [10] By using their own cars and drivers, Doob and Gross were able to create a large number of situations in which a car didn't move when the light turned green. Both Doob and Gross, as well as this author in a later study, [11] found that men who were stuck behind the unmoving car were much more likely to honk at the oblivious driver. Women drivers were not totally averse to honking (as indicated by the fact that more than 50% of the women drivers in both studies did honk), but they were less frequent in their aggressive honking than men were.

Other minor annoyances that occur in the course of a day's events may also lead to some display of aggression. How do you feel, for example, if someone bumps into you at a shopping center? Or how do you react if someone cuts in front of you while you are waiting in line for a movie? Social psychologist Mary Harris has conducted a series of studies that focus on just these occasions. In one such study, "experimenters" stepped in line in front of a randomly selected person, who afterward was considered the "subject."[12] The experimenter waited for approximately 20 seconds, observing the reactions of the subject, and then left the line. Both verbal and nonverbal responses by subjects were recorded. "Get the hell out of here" would be coded as a verbally aggressive response, to cite one example. Frowns, obscene gestures, and physical shoves were scored as forms of nonverbal aggression. If a subject either was polite or simply ignored the intruding experimenter, then no aggression was recorded. In this study, male and female subjects did not differ significantly in the amount of overall aggression they displayed toward the intruder. Women, however, were more likely to show nonverbal aggression than were men, primarily in the form of a glare. In another study that looked at people's responses to being bumped by a stranger in a shopping center, Harris again found that men and women did not differ in their tendency to act aggressively toward the bumper.[13]

What do these various findings tell us about the aggressive behavior of men and women? Can we conclude, as many have assumed, that men are more aggressive than women? The results certainly don't give consistent evidence of such a difference. In fact, at first glance, the results may seem quite contradictory.

Yet these contradictions may be understandable if we refer to the previous distinction between initiation and reaction. As in the case of altruism, some situations require the person to make the first move—to initiate the action rather than respond to the action of another. In the Buss situation, for example, the subject can give a passive learner a shock, even though that person has not previously shocked the subject.[14] Even when a third party is providing guidelines, the issue is still one of the individual male or female performing the first aggressive action. Men are more aggressive when this initiation is required. Honking horns would also fit into this initiation category. While the stalled driver may have frustrated the person behind, that driver has not directly confronted the person with an aggressive display, and men are again more likely to show aggression in this situation.

In contrast, other situations call for the subject to respond directly to aggressive behavior by another person. In the Taylor and Epstein laboratory study, for example, the subject receives a shock from the other student and is able to respond in kind. As we have seen, women become just as aggressive as men in this situation. In the same fashion, when someone cuts directly in front of a woman in line, that woman is no less aggressive than a man in her response—and on a nonverbal level, even more aggressive. Men show more aggression if an initiating response is required but no more than women when a reaction is in order.

We might also speculate that in any longer-term encounter when people have repeated opportunities to interact, aggression differences between men and women would be minimal. After the initial aggressive action, further behaviors could be interpreted as reactions to a provocation. In support of this speculation, sociologist Murray Straus has conducted many investigations of violence between husbands and wives, and these investigations suggest that aggressive acts occur equally frequently for the two partners.[15] Male aggression may only be at the tip of the iceberg.

MEN AND WOMEN AS VICTIMS

While the behavior of men and women as aggressors shows some interesting differences related to the situation, research dealing with men and women as the target of aggression is more consistent. Men get it more. In considering the research on altruism, we noticed that women tend to be helped more often than men. If there are norms that women should be protected more carefully, then it is probably not surprising to learn that people show less aggression toward a woman.

In the laboratory studies of Buss, for example, a "teacher" will administer less shock to a female "learner" than to a male.[16] The same pattern occurs in the study of Taylor and Epstein, even though the female in this case has an opportunity to return the shock to her partner.[17] Despite this provocation, both male and female subjects restrain themselves. Men tend to say (or yell) things like "I just can't hurt a girl." And even "girls," who are willing to retaliate against their unchivalrous male partner, show little inclination to shock another woman.

In the same way, Mary Harris has found that women line-cutters and body-bumpers are less likely to provoke aggression from their victims than are men.[18] One exception to this trend is the case of horn-honking. A woman driver stopped at the light is much more likely to get honked at by either the man or woman driver behind her.[19] This reversal is a little suprising, but it may be that the stereotype of the "damn woman driver" is a very strong one—strong enough, perhaps, to make honking at her a socially acceptable form of behavior.

For the most part, however, if all things are equal, men will be the target of more aggression than women. Yet all else is not always equal. Neither all men nor all women look the same. And in terms of women's "protective shield" against aggression, research has shown that the characteristics of the woman can alter the protective quality of the shielding norms.

Two psychologists at the University of Texas, Robert Kaleta and Arnold Buss, were interested in how the characteristics of the "victim" would affect the amount of aggression that a male college student would display.[20] A female college student served as a confederate victim and varied her appearance and her behavior so that she appeared more or less feminine in various conditions. In the *feminine appearance* condition, the young woman was neatly made up and wore a colorful frilly dress, along with nylon stockings and stylish shoes. In the *unfeminine appearance* condition, the same confederate used no makeup, pulled her hair back in a severe style, and wore baggy and rather sloppy clothes. In each of these appearance conditions, the behavior of the confederate varied, too. Half the time (*feminine behavior*) she appeared very feminine, asking polite questions and showing concern for the feelings of others. The other half of the time she acted oblivious to the concerns of others and was more assertive in her statements. Thus, the male subject, who was put in the position of giving shock to the young woman, saw one of four different degrees of femininity: one who acted feminine and looked feminine, one who looked feminine but didn't act particularly feminine, one who acted feminine but didn't look that way, or one who did neither. Did these differences in behavior and appearance affect the male subject's behavior? The answer is a clear yes. Women who were feminine in both behavior and appearance received the lowest shock intensities, while women who were unfeminine in both respects received the highest shock. Levels of aggression directed toward the other two types of women fell midway between these two extremes.

It appears that our society does have norms that say not to fight against women. An attractive woman apparently makes these norms more salient, as it did in the case of altruistic behavior. But if the woman in question has chosen to forsake some parts of the feminine role (by looking sloppy and acting assertive), there is more chance that the potential aggressor will also forsake some of his normative beliefs.

Looking at the situation from a different point of view, what if the potential aggressor doesn't believe in the traditional sex-role norms? Today many people are coming to believe in equality between the sexes and are rejecting the view that women should be submissive and protected. A group of psychologists at the University of Utah selected men on the basis of their attitudes toward women's roles and women's liberation. [21] One group of men (the Anti-Libs) favored traditional roles for women, whereas the other group (called Pro-Libs) believed in a more equalitarian role for women. The men in each of these groups were then put in a situation in which they could exchange blows with a female confederate using a pillow-like "club." In one part of the experiment, the female confederate simply defended herself but did not try to hit the subject. In a later phase of the experiment, she started to strike back. As the authors expected, the Pro-Libs showed much less reluctance to hit the young woman than did the Anti-Libs. These differences were strongest when the female confederate was simply defending herself. When she began to hit back, even the Anti-Libs showed some tendency to hit harder. Unfortunately, these experimenters did not include any conditions where men were allowed to hit men. As a result, we can't say whether the Pro-Libs were hitting women as much as they would hit men. We do know, however, that they hit women more than did men whose attitudes toward women were more traditional.

To summarize these findings, it does seem that as a general rule men are the targets of more aggression. Yet as is true of most general statements, this one is not without exception. Changes in the characteristics of the victim and in the attitudes of the potential aggressor will alter the simple generality so that women, as well as men, may get their share of attacks.

MEN AND WOMEN AS OBSERVERS OF AGGRESSION

What if a woman is not involved in the aggressive interchange but is simply a witness? The folklore on this point seems to provide us with contradictory clues. On the one hand, we might think that, because women are seen to represent passivity and nonaggressiveness, their presence should reduce the display of aggression. In Tennessee Williams' classic play *A Streetcar Named Desire,* Mitch firmly states that "poker should not be played in a house with women." Perhaps aggression is just a more extreme example of the same thing: "men's" activities should be done only in the presence of other men. "Fight in the street but not in the house" could be a practical suggestion to avoid damage, or it could be a recommendation not to be aggressive in the traditional "woman's place," the home. In contrast, however, some would argue that men fight to impress women with their strength and masculinity.[22] If this were the case, we would expect that the presence of a woman might actually increase aggression. Fortunately, there is some experimental evidence that helps us to answer this question.

Social psychologist Richard Borden set up a laboratory experiment in which male subjects interacted with a confederate in a competitive situation, during which they were able to select the level of shock they wanted their confederate-partner to receive.[23] While engaging in this battle, the subjects were observed by either a male or a female student who sat quietly in the same room. Borden's results showed that the subjects were much more aggressive if another male was watching them than if a female was witness. After a short period of time, the observer left the room. At this point, subjects who had been observed by a male showed a substantial decrease in their aggression, while the subjects who had been observed by a female showed little change. This evidence would suggest that neither of the folklore predictions considered above is quite accurate. The presence of a woman did not decrease the amount of aggression shown by subjects, as compared to when the competitors were by themselves. With another man watching, however, the male subjects showed a much higher level of aggressive behavior, suggesting that males may be more aggressive in an attempt either to impress the male or at least live up to the implied expectation of being "manly."

The subject himself could, of course, only guess at what the values of the observer were. Most people in this culture would probably assume that a man is more supportive of aggression than is a woman, and the results of Borden's first experiment are consistent with this assumption. In a second experiment, Borden made it easier for subjects to guess the values of the male or female observer. Some subjects in this second experiment saw an observer who was wearing a jacket with a karate patch and who mentioned that he or she had a brown belt in karate and very much enjoyed the sport. Other subjects met an observer who wore a SANE patch (Society Against Nuclear Expansion) and advocated pacifist goals. Under these conditions, both the values of the observer and his or her sex showed some effect on the aggressive responses of the subject, but the values were much more important. When the observer was a karate expert, the subject showed far more aggression than when the observer favored peaceful coexistence. In this second experiment, as in the first, the presence of presumably sympathetic observers served as a cue to increase aggressive behavior, but there was no evidence that the more pacifistic observer inhibited aggression as compared to an alone condition. More importantly, in terms of our present discussion, the presence of a woman encouraged aggression in the subject when it was clear that the woman herself supported aggression. In real-life situations, then, we could expect that the tough or aggressive woman would be as influential as a man in encouraging aggressive behavior in others. Only if it is known or assumed that the woman values nonviolence will less aggression be shown in her presence. And only if it is known or assumed that the man favors violent behavior will actors choose to behave more aggressively in his presence. If the evidence is lacking, we will probably rely on our stereotyped assumptions about what men and women are like. But if we are given more evidence, we will change our behavior to account for this new information.

Surveying the aggression literature, we find some clear patterns in the behavior of women and men. As in the case of altruism, the typical stereotypes of men and women appear to affect the aggressive behavior directed toward the sexes. Whereas women are helped more often, they are harmed less often. Information inconsistent with the stereotype will in turn alter the behavior, and the "unfeminine" woman loses her protective advantage.

As initiators, men are the more aggressive of the two sexes, consistent with the conclusions of many others. However, in contrast to Simone de Beauvoir's statement, women have not been totally deprived of the lessons of violence. Given provocations, women will show aggressive behavior on a par with men. Such findings suggest that the lessons have been learned, but the recitals are simply less frequent.

Chapter 9

Strategies of Interaction: Compliance, Cooperation, Competition, and Congeniality

*I think that when women are encouraged to be competitive,
too many of them become disagreeable.*

Dr. Benjamin Spock

*Competitiveness is not only emphasized as a desirable trait
in men but is seen as an absolute requirement for masculinity.*

Marc Feigen Fasteau

*When men and women agree, it is only in their
conclusions; their reasons are always different.*

George Santayana

In my present position, I am fortunate to have a colleague who,
as an ethologist, shares his farm with a pack of ten wolves (safely
surrounded by a large wire fence). Observing the behavior of these
wolves is a fascinating pastime. During hours of wolf-watching, I have
seen struggles for dominance, sharing of food, and good-natured
play, and the translations to human behavior are often tempting to
make. Like wolves, we can adopt many strategies in our interaction
with others. In a chess game, for example, our only goal may be to
win, while a bicycle built for two may foster cooperation. On other
occasions our behavior may represent compliance with an authority
or an attempt to establish ties of friendship. In the previous two
chapters, we considered some specific forms of interaction, namely
offering help and rendering harm. Our concern in this chapter will be
the more general strategies that men and women use in their
interactions with one another: the behaviors of compliance, cooperation, competition, and congeniality.

CONFORMITY AND COMPLIANCE

Early studies of compliance suggested that women, like subordinate wolves, were always more likely to give in. A survey of the
attitude-change studies conducted in the 1950s, for example, led

Janis and Field to conclude that women are more persuasible than men,[1] and this conclusion has persisted for many years. A related assumption has been that women will always show more conformity, adapting to a group's opinion even when that opinion may be incorrect. This assumption was based on early studies conducted by Solomon Asch, in which subjects were asked to select two lines that are equal in length after hearing the judgment of a group of peers.[2] Interpretations of these apparent differences between men and women have stressed the greater willingness of women to go along with the opinion of another and to be docile in the face of disagreement. Yet despite the widespread acceptance of this sex difference, more recent investigations show that such a ready assumption of greater female compliance may often be in error.

Recall from Chapter 8, for example, that women were less likely to follow the orders of an experimenter than were men, when the orders required administering shock to a passive learner. Many other exceptions have been reported in recent years as well.[3] One possible explanation for this shift in findings is that women have changed over the past decade. While this possibility cannot be discounted, there is a less transitory explanation that points again to the importance of specific tasks and situations. We learned earlier that men generally excel in tasks requiring visual-spatial abilities. When we discover that the studies finding conformity differences between men and women generally use spatial tasks, we begin to suspect that the nature of the task could be a critical factor.

Frank Sistrunk and John McDavid harbored similar suspicions and designed an experiment to test this possibility directly.[4] They first compiled a list of topics that could be sorted reliably into three groups: issues of greater interest to men, issues of greater interest to women, and issues that interest both sexes equally. They then asked a group of students to give their opinions on 15 different topics from each group. Furthermore, they placed conformity pressures on these students by giving them the opinions of a fictitious majority for each question. By comparing the subject's response to that of the fictitious group opinion, the investigators could measure how much each subject conformed to each type of topic.

The results of this study are remarkably clear. On feminine topics, men showed more conformity than women, and on masculine topics, women conformed more than men. When the topics were neutral, there was no difference in the conformity of men and women. Judging from these results, we would be greatly in error if we assumed that compliance is a typical mode of interaction for women. Both men and women may be influenced by the judgments of others, and both may choose to go along with the crowd. It is possible, of course, that men are confident in more topic areas than women are. If this is true, then women will still be seen conforming more often. Nonetheless, the basic strategy of men and women is the same: both sexes show independence in familiar areas and conformity when the territory is unfamiliar.

COOPERATION AND COMPETITION

While some situations in our lives may present pressures to comply with the wishes or opinions of another person, other types of interaction require us to work in concert with another individual. You and a friend may decide to build a boat, for example, and will need to develop strategies for working together so that the best possible boat can be built. Other situations may put you in direct competition with one another. For example, you and the student that you always study with both enroll in a class, and the professor says only one A will be given. If both of you aspire to the A, then new study arrangements may be necessary. These pressures for cooperation and competition are a common experience for most of us.

The major method of studying cooperation and competition within the laboratory has been a game called the *Prisoner's Dilemma*. The original anecdote on which the game is based varies in the telling, but in one version two prisoners and a manipulative district attorney are the principal characters. Each prisoner is a likely suspect for a recent crime, but the D.A. needs a confession. He* gives each prisoner two choices: confess or don't confess. If both prisoners refuse to confess, the D.A. admits that he will have to release them both for lack of evidence. On the other hand, if both prisoners confess, the D.A. says that he will convict them both, although the sentences will be lenient. In contrast, if only one prisoner confesses, the D.A. promises that the prisoner who confesses will be released and will be given a reward for supplying state's evidence, while the book will be thrown at the nonconfessing prisoner. Thus, the dilemma.

This game is often called a *mixed-motive game,* because two competing motives are presumably involved. If the prisoner is concerned only about himself (an individualistic motive), the choice of confessing is clearly better. At best (if the other prisoner refuses

---

*Not surprisingly, this traditional story has always referred to the principal characters as traditional "he's."

to confess), he will be released and receive a reward as well, and at worst he will get a short sentence. Yet if our hypothetical prisoner is concerned about the welfare of the other prisoner as well as himself (a cooperative motive), then he should refuse to confess and hope that his partner does the same.

The translation of this anecdote to an experimental setting results in some lack of urgency. Rather than being concerned with prison terms and freedom, subjects in the laboratory experiment are concerned with pennies or with hypothetical points. The cooperative choice in this translation means, for example, that both players will win 1¢. By defecting (being concerned only about one's own fate), a person may win 2¢. Another alteration in the laboratory setting is the duration. Rather than making a single crucial choice, subjects are asked to make as many as 300 of these choices in a consecutive sequence. Also, in most cases it is left up to the players to figure out the implications of making one or the other choice in terms of an ultimate payoff, and the experimenters simply assume that each player will try to get the largest payoff possible.

Accepting for the moment the social scientist's definition of cooperation, what do we find men and women doing in this situation? Initially, men and women behave identically in the Prisoner's Dilemma game. In the first set of trials, both sexes select the "cooperative" response about half of the time. Essentially, people seem to be trying out both possible responses to see what happens. Over the course of several dozen or several hundred trials, however, differences between men and women become apparent. Men typically show either no change or a slight increase in their choice of the cooperative response, while women show a decline.[5] On the basis of these findings, many Prisoner's Dilemma advocates have concluded that women are less cooperative than men.

Such a finding may seem a bit surprising, given the stereotyped assumptions that men are more competitive than women. One possibility is, of course, that the stereotypes are wrong. Yet a more likely possibility is that the Prisoner's Dilemma is not the ideal paradigm for observing cooperative and competitive behavior. It is not at all clear that subjects perceive the cooperating and defecting strategies in the same way that the experimenter does. Although mathematical probabilities can demonstrate that the maximum payoff for each individual player will result if both players choose the "cooperative" response, it is quite likely that the subject without a pocket computer has not figured out these mathematical probabilities. Social psychologist Charlan Nemeth has made a strong case against the Prisoner's Dilemma, arguing that for the most part subjects simply don't understand what they are doing in it.[6] In fact, she describes one investigator who was brave enough to ask his subjects what their motives actually were and who discovered that virtually none of the subjects felt they had been cooperating. If this is true, then we really haven't made much progress in understanding cooperation and competition, let alone how these motives differ among men and women.

Part of the difficulty is that, given only two choices, each choice can satisfy a number of possible motives on the part of the player. In choosing the "cooperative" response, for example, the player may be maximizing the ultimate payoff, behaving generously toward his or her partner by appearing to take a lesser payoff, or simply showing a disregard for payoffs in general. Similarly, in choosing the "defective" alternative, the subject may be trying to win more money or just attempting to beat the opponent. At least one study has tried to separate some of these various motives by offering players several different games that allow different motives to be satisfied. Bob Wyer and Christine Malinowski constructed a series of games in which they could separate individualistic motives from competitive motives.[7] Interestingly enough, there were no overall differences between men and women in their tendency to be either individualistic (maximize their own gains) or to be competitive (maximize their own gains while minimizing the opponent's gains). Differences did occur, however, depending on the sex of the players and their partners and on the relative competence of each player as established on a previous task. Men were more competitive against other men and against highly competent players as a general rule; however, a man who was himself low in previous achievement became highly competitive when playing against a woman with a previous record of achievement. (Perhaps the man, no matter how bad his performance, is reluctant to be topped by a woman.) In contrast, women tended to be more competitive when playing against low achievers of either sex. These women may have had lower expectations (as we saw in Chapter 4), and only against an incompetent partner did they feel capable of some success.

The Wyer and Malinowski study, although it still uses the rather artificial framework of the Prisoner's Dilemma, nonetheless takes some steps in a positive direction to separate possible motives that may be intertwined in the more standard Prisoner's Dilemma game. Their study also suggests that characteristics of the opponent can make a difference. Thus, before totally abandoning the Prisoner's Dilemma paradigm, let's look at a few other studies that, although maintaining the two-choice pattern, have included other variables that seem to alter players' responses. Perhaps in looking at how the behaviors are changed, we can gain some clues to what motives may be operating. Arnold Kahn and his colleagues considered the attractiveness of the player's partner and found that men and women responded differently.[8] While the attractiveness of their partner made no difference to men in terms of their game behavior, women increased their "cooperative" choices when their male partner was attractive. In fact, with an attractive partner, women showed the same level of cooperation as did the men. These results suggest that men are relatively insensitive to the interpersonal aspects of the game, concentrating instead on their strategy of play. Women, in contrast, will alter their play depending on the appearance of their partner, increasing their cooperation as the attractiveness of the partner increases.

There are other differences in the way men and women play this game and perhaps differences in what the game means to the players. Joseph Hottes and Arnold Kahn allowed partners (who were always of the same sex) to talk to each other after they had played the game for some period of time.[9] When the authors analyzed these conversations, they found that men frequently talked about strategy, and in their subsequent playing they made more cooperative responses, which gave them a higher joint payoff. Women, however, almost never discussed strategy in these sessions. Instead, they talked of roommates, common friends, and their general interest in the game (or lack thereof). Following these conversations, the women showed little change in their game style. Other studies show that men and women act differently when their opponent can retaliate against them. In this situation, women become much more cooperative than do men.[10]

The Prisoner's Dilemma studies have yielded a number of intriguing sex differences. These findings may well point to differences between men and women in their strategies of interaction. However, in my mind these results tell us less about cooperation and competition per se than about different interaction strategies used by the two sexes. Men seem to be more oriented toward the game itself, attempting to develop tactics that will guarantee them the largest financial payoff. In part, this may be a function of the task itself. Men's greater interest in mathematical tasks may predispose them to take the game more seriously. Women on the other hand seem less concerned with the game itself and more concerned with the interpersonal setting. Alterations in their partner's appearance lead to an alteration in play, and opportunities for conversation are used to establish more interpersonal contacts. These different orientations may give us some important clues about the behavior of women and men, quite apart from the original intentions of the Prisoner's Dilemma game.

FORMING COALITIONS

Similar patterns of sex differences in interaction strategies can be seen in studies of coalition formation, where the most prominent investigator is Edgar Vinacke. [11] The basic situation in his series of experiments involves three people playing a game of Parcheesi, in which one or more players try to reach "home" first. However, in most instances, the players do not have an equal chance to win. Vinacke sets up differences in the relative strength of each player by varying how many spaces each person can move on the roll of a single die. To counter these uneven weights, players can form coalitions that allow them to move their markers in tandem simultaneously (like "kings" in checkers) and share the winner's prize. The question then becomes how players will form coalitions in order to improve their chances of winning.

When the three players in this game are all men, Vinacke has found that the men will play competitively, with an apparently strong motive to win. To accomplish this goal, each player will attempt to form an alliance that will ensure his winning the game. Groups of all women, on the other hand, act differently. They try to achieve the best outcome for all players, so that, in spite of the initial distribution of weights, each player will have a fair share of the final prize. Vinacke has also considered what happens when men and women are together in groups of three, with either men or women being in the majority. Again, there is a general trend for men to form alliances in order to maximize their own gains, while women form alliances in order to minimize the others' (and their own) losses. A single woman also shows a tendency to ally with one of the other two men, even when her own position is strong enough to win without an alliance, whereas the man in a parallel situation does not make a similar alliance. Perhaps of even greater interest in Vinacke's study of mixed-sex coalitions is the fact that women, whether in the minority or majority, do as well as or better than men in terms of total points earned. Thus, while the woman's strategy is a less competitive one, it is no less effective.

At one level, the results of the coalition studies appear to contradict the Prisoner's Dilemma findings. In the latter case, investigators have claimed that men are more cooperative, but coalition studies show the opposite. (In Vinacke's terms, men use an exploitative strategy, and women use an accommodative strategy.) While both of these situations are somewhat removed from the cooperation and competition of everyday life, the coalition studies seem to be a much clearer problem situation for subjects. Unlike the Prisoner's Dilemma game, subjects in coalition studies understand the implications of various strategies. At another level, however, the findings of the two paradigms are quite similar. In both cases, women are showing a greater concern for the interpersonal aspects of the situation, preferring to establish bonds of friendship rather than alliances that are geared toward maximizing the payoff.

Although women appear less concerned with maximizing their financial payoff, the results of Vinacke's studies showed that the female strategy was no less effective in terms of points earned. How important is the monetary payoff for women? Is it a primary goal or just a secondary fringe benefit of an interpersonal strategy?

DIVIDING REWARDS: THE NORM OF EQUITY

A number of social scientists have been interested in how men and women will reward themselves and their partners when they are involved in a mutual problem-solving situation. The model for these experiments is quite simple. Two people work on a problem, and then the experimenter gives the partners a chance to divide the reward between themselves in any way that they choose. A basic theory in social psychology predicts that equity should be the rule used in dividing the reward. Recall our earlier discussion of equity in Chapter 3, where we were concerned with how an outside observer would reward a performance. In the present case, we're talking about two people dividing a reward among themselves, but the basic principle remains the same. The player who contributes more to the solution should get more of the reward.

If you ask people to imagine themselves in a variety of hypothetical situations, both men and women will say that equitable situations are the fairest. For example, if you are told to imagine that you are more valuable to your employer than your co-worker is and that you make more money per hour than your co-worker, would you think that situation was fair? What if you felt you were more valuable than your co-worker but were receiving lower pay than your co-worker? When psychologists have studied these kinds of hypothetical situations, they have found that most men and women agree that the first situation is fair, while the second one is not.[12]

As social psychologists have often discovered, however, the things that people imagine they might do are not always the same things that they actually do when the real situation occurs. In a real situation involving rewards, men and women do not act the same. Consider the following situation. You are told that you will be working with another person of the same sex. Although you will be in separate rooms, each of you will work on a series of multiplication problems. At the end of a ten-minute period, the experimenter will award your team some money, based on the total number of problems that the two of you have solved. At the end of the ten minutes, the experimenter says your team has won $1.45, and you will be allowed to decide how much money you receive and how much your partner should receive. At the same time, the experimenter tells you that you solved 37 problems, while your partner solved only 22 problems. How would you divide the reward? Social psychologists Gerald Leventhal and Douglas Lane found that in the situation just described men tend to follow an equity rule.[13] On the average, the men in their study kept 61% of the money for themselves and gave 39% to their inferior partner. If the situation were reversed and the other player had the superior performance, men kept 42% of the reward for themselves and gave 58% to their partner. These choices seem to indicate that equity is operating: the player who solves more problems is awarded more of the money.

Women, in contrast, did not act in quite the same way. When they were told they were the better player, women kept only 53% of the reward for themselves and gave 47% to their partner. On the other hand, when they were the inferior player, they were even less generous to themselves than men were, keeping only 34% of the reward while giving 66% to their partner. In both winning and losing situations, women appeared to be more "humble" than men. Some writers have suggested that women may be operating by a different norm—the norm of equality. The equality norm would suggest that rewards should be divided equally among players, no matter how much each person has contributed to the final outcome. In this kind of "one for all and all for one" strategy, people may assume that each person contributed as much as he or she could and is therefore entitled to an equal share of the reward. Yet if women are going by this rule of equality, they seem to be doing it only when they are the better performer. When they are the inferior performer, their behavior is in line with an equity notion, though they are harder on themselves than men are. There was some evidence in this experiment by Leventhal and Lane that women were using a different norm in the two situations. While men in both inferior and superior conditions said that they had taken their performance into account when deciding on the reward, women said they did not consider performance much when they had done better than their partner but considered it very strongly when they had done poorly.

Several other investigators have found the same patterns of behavior by men and women when they are dividing rewards.[14] Yet most of these studies have used same-sex pairs, and as in the case of some of the earlier helping studies, we can't tell whether it is the sex of the allocator or the sex of the recipient that is causing the difference. Women may be more humble (or accommodative) than men; on the other hand, perhaps everyone is more generous to a female partner than to a male partner. Conveniently, Larry Messé and Charlene Callahan have solved this problem for us in a recent study. By using same-sex pairs as well as mixed-sex pairs, they found (as is so often the case) that both explanations are partly true.[15] Women are more generous than men toward their partner, whether that partner is a male or a female. (In both instances, Messé and Callahan found that women kept approximately 55% of the reward when they themselves had the superior performance.) Men varied their behavior according to the sex of their partner: with another male, men kept 64% of the reward for themselves, but when they were working with a woman, men kept only 54% for themselves. Perhaps this situation brings out some of the altruistic motives in men, for as we have seen earlier men tend to be more altruistic, and women tend to be the recipients of more altruistic offers. Alternatively, men may be attempting to establish a positive interpersonal relationship with the woman by showing this generosity, a motive women may display more consistently.

The question still remains, however, why men and women respond differently when they are asked to reward themselves and a partner. A number of explanations have been suggested, and we might consider how well each explanation fits the available data.

First, there is the argument that women operate on an equality principle rather than an equity principle. While the behavior of women who have a superior performance seems to agree with this (as do the coalition studies), we've seen that equality is not the rule when women have an inferior performance. Furthermore, there are a number of studies showing that, when women are giving rewards to two other people and not to themselves, they follow the same equity patterns as do men.[16] Thus, a simple equality explanation does not seem to be the answer.

A second explanation for sex differences in equity behavior is based on some of the research presented in Chapter 4 on the self-evaluation patterns of men and women. As we saw in that earlier discussion, men tend to rate their performance more favorably than do women over a wide variety of situations. Particularly in the case of failure, we find women downgrading their estimates of their own ability and performance level. It is possible, then, that when women are asked to divide a reward between themselves and their partner they do assess relative inputs as equity theory would suggest. However, if women have a general tendency to undervalue their own performance (or if men have a general tendency to overvalue their performance), then women would perceive that they had less input than men would. Consequently, they would reward themselves less than would men. The basis of this argument is that subjective estimates of input differ from those objective facts that the experimenter supplies. Direct evidence for this link between self-evaluation and reward is minimal and mixed,[17] but it should be considered a reasonable possibility.

A third explanation for the sex differences in reward behavior is that women see less connection between their performance and financial reward than do men. In the employment setting, for example, it has been suggested that women may voluntarily accept lower salaries because they do not see their work so directly connected to pay as do men.[18] The perception could be related to the traditional roles men and women have filled, whereby many typical women's jobs (for example, cooking and cleaning) do not have a monetary reward.

Within the laboratory, there are a number of studies that do show women less concerned with the financial aspects of the situation. First of all, when directly asked, women will say that the money is less important.[19] Promises of rewards also have more effect on the performance of men than woman,[20] and women will more readily sacrifice money in order to preserve face in an embarrassing situation.[21] Thus, there is a fairly strong basis for concluding that women, where their own behavior is concerned, make less connection between performance and reward.

Suggesting less of a connection does not mean that there is no connection at all. Furthermore, women may respond much like men when another person does the allocating. In one study that dealt specifically with these reactions, Arnold Kahn allowed subjects to divide money with a partner after they had been either underpaid, overpaid, or equitably paid by that same partner.[22] In the overpaid and equitably paid conditions, men and women acted exactly the same. They split the money evenly with a partner who had split the money evenly with them, and they gave themselves a smaller share of the reward when their partner had overpaid them on the previous exchange. When subjects were underpaid by their partner, however, men and women responded somewhat differently. Although both sexes kept a proportionately larger share of the money for themselves in the next exchange, men kept significantly more than women did.

If women do see less connection between performance and financial reward, we might ask if there are links between performance and some other forms of reward. This question brings us back to the general topic of interpersonal strategies and the differing behavior of women and men. It seems quite likely that in the reward-allocation studies women are concerned with the interpersonal aspects as well as the financial. Overpaying one's opponent may be viewed as a means of creating a friendship, particularly if one believes that the other person values money. In the same way that women show accommodation strategies in the coalition studies, they may be attempting to accommodate their partner in the reward setting. Financial reward becomes secondary to social reward. [23]

Our survey of the interpersonal exchange in the laboratory points to consistent patterns in the behavior of women and men. Contrary to some beliefs, these patterns do not show men merely dominating and women acceding to the wishes of others. Simple compliance is not characteristic of either sex. What we do find in these interactions is a difference in the objectives. Men in general adopt problem-focused strategies concerned with winning the prize, gaining the money, and surpassing the opponent. Women, in contrast, seem more concerned with the interpersonal aspects of these situations, attempting to establish relationships with the players rather than victories in the games. While the outcome of these two strategies may in many instances be the same, the reasons, as Santayana suggested, are different.

Chapter 10

Women and Men in Groups

Two women placed together makes cold weather.

Shakespeare

The male bond and the male interactions underlie the anatomical and physiological growth processes of communities.

Lionel Tiger

Anthropologist Lionel Tiger has suggested that one of the strongest and most basic elements in any society is the relationship among men in groups. Men "bond" together, Tiger says, and these bonds are very different from those that form between men and women or between women and women. For Tiger, these bonds have a hereditary base: the bonding in human males evolved from earlier animal behavior, was strengthened with the development of all-male hunting parties, and continues to be played out in politics and war. In fact, Tiger would argue that the existence of these male bonds is essential for the maintenance of a society.[1]

In previous chapters, we've looked at the interactions of dyads—two people acting together or in opposition to one another. In this chapter, we'll broaden this focus to the study of women and men in groups, attempting to learn, among other things, whether the speculations of Tiger are valid. You might consider for a moment the groups to which you have belonged or groups that you have observed. Do all-male groups have a greater sense of camaraderie and commitment than all-female groups? Do sororities and fraternities mean different things to their members? Who becomes the leader of these groups? These are some of the questions that we'll consider in this chapter.

WHO JOINS GROUPS?

The social psychologist's study of groups typically deals with a number of individuals who are artificially merged into a group once they arrive at the psychology laboratory for their required experimental participation. More ambitious psychological studies have focused on intact groups, often in the military services, and sometimes in exotic settings such as Sealab, a capsule 80 feet under the surface of the Pacific Ocean.[2] While these studies are abundant, the findings are not particularly useful for our present concerns. First, these groups are not entirely voluntary, and second, the groups are primarily male. It is thus difficult for the social psychologist to respond to Tiger's contentions that males are more likely to "bond," or to form groups.

Fortunately, sociologists are more tuned in to the patterns of real-life group formation, and a recent study by Alan Booth gives us some basis against which to test Tiger's hypotheses about the greater tendency of men to join groups.[3] Booth interviewed 800 adults who lived in either Lincoln or Omaha, Nebraska, asking them about their friends, relatives, and group memberships. All of these adults were at least 45 years of age, and we can assume that by this age the respondents had developed fairly stable patterns of group behavior. Booth asked the men and women he interviewed who their friends were and how close they felt to each of these friends, as well as how close they felt to their relatives. He also asked them to what organizations they belonged and how much time they spent on the activities of these organizations each month.

The results of this study give little support to Tiger's argument that men's groups are more numerous or that male bonding is stronger. Males reported only slightly more close friends than did women (3.9 versus 3.6 on the average), and in direct opposition to Tiger's argument, men reported having more friends of the opposite sex than did women. Although the percentage of opposite-sexed friends was low for both sexes (15% for males and 9% for females), this difference was statistically significant and would indicate that women have a stronger propensity for same-sex pairing. Booth also obtained several indications of the strength of the friendship bonds, and in each case the results suggest that the bonds between women may be stronger. Women were more likely to have weekly contact with their close friends, engaged in more spontaneous activities with their friends, and confided in their friends more often. (In an interesting parallel of these findings, lawyer Marc Fasteau has discussed friendships between men in his book *The Male Machine,* and he suggests that men always have to have a specific reason for getting together. Women, he observes, feel more free to just get together.)[4]

In terms of group participation, Booth found that women did belong to somewhat fewer voluntary organizations than did men. Yet in terms of the average number of hours spent, women scored higher, suggesting that women's commitment to these groups may if anything be higher. Finally, perhaps most directly speaking to Tiger's argument, this study found that there was no difference between men and women in their tendency to belong to groups of a single sex.

These findings may not provide a final answer on the question of who joins groups. Cross-sex friendships, for example, may be much more common among both men and women in their 20s than among men and women in their 40s. Furthermore, we need to compare women and men who have equal occupational responsibilities. Women who are past the child-bearing years, for example, may simply have more time to devote to voluntary organizations than do men who are employed in 40-hour-per-week jobs. Far more extensive research is needed, covering not only formal organizations and immediate friendships but also sports groups, men's and women's consciousness-raising groups, encounter and therapy groups—in other words, the full range of group-interaction possibilities. Yet this preliminary evidence indicates that Tiger may not have the final word.

GROUP ROLES AND GROUP PARTICIPATION

Let's turn from the cities of Nebraska to research laboratories across the continent to see what social psychologists have found out about the behavior of men and women in groups (recalling that these are groups generally assembled by an experimenter rather than emerging out of a natural context). We have seen in earlier chapters that men and women differ in their styles of communication and their strategies of interaction. Do these differences show up when men and women have the opportunity to interact together in a group situation?

In a classic study designed to consider different group roles, social psychologists Fred Strodtbeck and Richard Mann formed groups of men and women that very closely resembled real-life, rather than laboratory, situations.[5] Using the jury rolls of Chicago and St. Louis, these investigators arranged for groups of twelve potential jurors to meet together, read transcripts of a trial, and then to deliberate and reach a verdict on the case. During these highly realistic group interactions, all of the exchanges among the simulated jurors were recorded, and Strodtbeck and Mann were able to analyze the form of interchange that took place between the men and women of the jury. Using previously constructed procedures for analyzing the group interchange, the investigators could separate verbal behavior into two basic categories. *Instrumental* acts in such a group setting include comments in which the speaker gives an opinion or offers information. *Expressive* responses are less concerned with the task per se and more concerned with the group feelings. Examples of this latter category are comments that indicate group solidarity, show a release of tension, and offer agreement with the suggestions of another group member. The conversations by Strodtbeck and Mann's juries showed a clear split along sex lines: men were much more likely to make comments that could be considered instrumental, while women's comments more frequently fell in the expressive category.

Although these investigators found sharp differences between men and women, we must always consider the effect that changes in the culture may have on the patterns observed at a particular time and place. Since 1956 (when Strodtbeck and Mann did their study), many aspects of the culture have changed, and it is possible that the findings of Strodtbeck and Mann would not hold true in a more contemporary setting. However, the same patterns have been found in the 1970s. Quite recently, Jane Piliavin and Rachel Martin conducted a study of group behavior with students at the University of Wisconsin.[6] Like Strodtbeck and Mann, Piliavin and Martin found that women gave more comments that could be classified as expressive or socioemotional, while men made more comments of an instrumental nature.

In addition to simply replicating the earlier findings for mixed-sex groups, Piliavin and Martin were also curious about what goes on in groups composed solely of one sex and how these groups compare to mixed-sex groups. In earlier studies of group behavior, it has often been found that both the instrumental role and the expressive role will emerge in group discussion and that both may actually be necessary for successful group functioning. Thus, in a group of men, some men would be expected to take the socioemotional role. Similarly, in a group of women, some women should adopt the instrumental role. Piliavin and Martin reasoned that, if these dual needs exist in a group, then women in all-women groups should show more instrumental behaviors than women in mixed-sex groups. Although the instrumental behaviors presumably are needed in both groups, in the mixed-sex groups there would be men present to assume their more typical instrumental role. In the same way, these authors expected that men would show less expressive behavior in a mixed-sex group than in an all-male group, because in the latter there would not be women present to pick up on the expressive needs of the group. While these predictions seem quite reasonable, the results showed almost the opposite to be true. Women showed more instrumental behavior and less expressive behavior when they were in the mixed-sex group than when they were in an all-women group. Males, in contrast, showed some tendency to be more expressive in mixed-sex groups than in all-male groups. Analysis of negative comments made by group members showed interesting changes as well. When in a mixed group, men disagreed less, showed less tension, and seemed friendlier than when they were with only men. Women, on the other hand, disagreed more in the mixed-sex group than in their same-sex groups but showed little difference on the other two indicants.[7]

Apparently, groups composed of both men and women allow all of the members more options. Instead of increasing flexibility, groups of just one sex seem to limit or polarize the members in more traditional interaction patterns. Perhaps such limitations reflect the fact that men and women have become accustomed to using a single style, and the alternatives do not occur when only their own sex is present. At the same time, however, this use of limited alternatives would suggest that single-sex groups are not the most successful. If, as earlier investigators have suggested, both instrumental and expressive roles are necessary for a group to operate well, then it would follow that a mixed-sex group would be preferable in most cases.

One additional aspect of the Piliavin and Martin study deserves mention. In a second phase of the experiment, the experimenters selected one "target person" and attempted to modify that person's discussion behavior. Briefly, this modification was done by presenting a series of red and green lights that were supposed to represent the experimenter's evaluation of the individual's performance. In actual fact, the experimenter gave the target person a green light whenever he or she said something, providing consistently positive reinforcement for all of that person's contributions. Whenever the target person was silent, a red light was shown. After these reinforcement procedures, the experimenters observed the behavior of the target person in a subsequent group-discussion period. Interesting things happened. When a female in a mixed-sex group was the target, not only did she increase her overall participation but also both men and women in the group became less stereotyped in their behaviors, each showing equal amounts of both task and socio-emotional contributions. In contrast, when a male was chosen as the target person, both men and women increased their tendencies toward stereotyped contributions. Essentially, the male as target person seems to have reinforced the standard patterns of interaction, and both sexes simply solidified their behaviors along these lines. On the other hand, when a woman was being reinforced, there was a shift from the standard pattern: both the target woman and other women in the group began to show more instrumental behaviors, and the men tried out more socioemotional options. This finding suggests that, while the communication patterns of men and women may be ingrained, they are not immutable. Under certain circumstances, both sexes may show an increase in their range of alternatives.

CROWDED GROUPS

An intriguing direction taken by recent research on group behavior is a consideration of the effects of crowding. Overpopulation and urban density have become important ecological issues in recent years, and a number of highly publicized studies done with rats have suggested that population density results in aggression, social pathology, and eventual death. Observers have been quick to generalize these results to explain urban crime and riots. Yet in fact we know relatively little about the effects of crowding itself, as opposed to the multiple effects of unemployment, lack of education, limited finances, and other similar causes that can easily contribute to an increase in aggression and crime.

Recently, social scientists, often in conjunction with experts from other fields, have taken some initial steps toward determining just what the effects of crowding on human behavior are. Does crowding cause decrements in performance? Do people become more aggressive or more friendly? Do men and women differ in their reactions to a crowded situation?

Before attempting to provide answers to these questions, we should first define some basic terms. Perhaps the central concept is *density,* which refers to the number of people per unit of area. Thus, the density would be greater when ten people were in a room 5' x 5' (2.5 square feet per person) than when the same ten people were in a room 10' x 10' (10 square feet per person). *Group size* simply refers to the number of people in a group, no matter what the size or shape of the room is. Unfortunately, some of the early investigators of crowding behavior tended to vary these two factors simultaneously. For example, to study a low-density condition, the experimenters would place ten people in a 100-square-foot room. To study high density, they would place 25 people in that same room. While it is clear that density was being varied in such studies, it is equally clear that group size was being varied as well. This confusion of the two concepts is important because earlier research on basic group processes has suggested that the size of a group affects people's reactions to that group. Generally, people express more positive feelings for a group and its members when the group is smaller rather than larger. Thus, when these earlier investigators found people to be more negative when there were 25 bodies in a 100-square-foot room, they could not be certain whether it was simply the number of people or the density that caused negative feelings.

With these basic concepts in hand, let's turn to the recent research. On the basis of the material covered in Chapter 6, we might even be able to make some predictions about the reactions of men and women to conditions of density. Because we know that men generally prefer a larger personal space separating them from others than do women, we might predict that men would find crowded situations more unpleasant than would women.

The initial studies of density have indeed supported this prediction. Social psychologist Jonathan Freedman and his colleagues found that when single-sexed groups of seven or eight were asked to act as individual jurors in either high- or low-density conditions, the sexes differed.[8] Men reacted more negatively in the high-density condition (and gave more severe sentences to the mock defendent). Women did just the opposite, viewing the high-density conditions as more pleasant than low-density conditions. When Freedman then looked at groups that had both men and women in the same group, he found that density had no effect on the feelings of the group members.

Other investigators have found similar results, supporting the idea that men are more uncomfortable than women in highly crowded conditions.[9] Andrew Schettino and Richard Borden have provided an ingenious demonstration of sex differences and crowding in the natural setting of a college classroom.[10] These investigators asked students enrolled in classes at the beginning of a semester to respond to a brief questionnaire about their general feelings—how good, secure, nervous, crowded, and aggressive they felt. By using classes of various sizes (ranging from 13 to 279), Schettino and Borden were able to analyze the students' feelings in terms of group size and density. The most interesting aspects of their data were the findings for aggressiveness: men reported feeling increasingly aggressive as density of the classroom increased, while women's feelings on this dimension did not vary with the density of the room. Among women, nervousness was more strongly related to density than was aggressiveness. These findings support the conclusion that men and women may respond quite differently to the experience of being crowded.

Despite these consistent findings, other recent evidence suggests that we can't automatically assume that men will always be more negative in high-density conditions. Not only group size, as mentioned earlier, but also the time that a group is together may be important influences on the behavior of men and women in groups. For instance, being on a crowded elevator for a few minutes, while not the most pleasant experience in the world, may be less unpleasant than being in an equally small space with several people for several hours. On the other hand, forced confinement over a long period of time could actually be fun—positive feelings could develop that might not happen in a shorter time period. As one example, we can think of reports from those who experienced New York City's famous blackout. After the initial fear was dispelled, many people reported that high-density confinement produced some terrific parties!

One step toward dealing with some of these complicating factors has been taken recently by Joan Marshall and Richard Heslin. [11] In their study of crowding, two different sizes of groups were studied (four persons and 16 persons) as well as two different levels of density (either 4 square feet per person or 17.5 square feet per person). The groups were either all male, all female, or had an equal number of males and females within the same group. The task subjects were asked to perform was a fairly complicated one, which lasted an hour and a half and required each member to participate. Briefly, subjects were asked to construct a paragraph, based on phrases that were divided equally among the members. The nice thing about this task was that, unlike some earlier experiments, subjects had to work together. Each member's contribution was necessary in order for the group to achieve the final product.

The results of this study are rather complicated but probably reflect the complexity of the situation we are trying to understand. As expected from earlier group research, members generally liked small groups better than large groups (though this tendency was far more pronounced for the men). Beyond this, the composition of the group made a difference. While men generally preferred mixed groups to all-male groups, no matter what the size, women showed a split in their preferences. If the group had both men and women, women preferred it to be large, while they were more positive about an all-female group when it was small. Density also had an effect. Both men and women liked being crowded when they were in mixed-sex groups (which may not surprise you if you're romantically inclined). When groups consisted of only one sex, in contrast, men preferred to be crowded and women preferred being uncrowded.

These results are indeed complicated, particularly when we compare them to earlier studies that showed men liking uncrowded settings and women liking crowded settings.

One possible explanation for these findings relates to the time involved in being together. Initially, or over a short time period, men may feel more negatively about being crowded than do women, consistent with the desire of men for a greater area of personal space. The lack of their normal space may create hostility in men (a kind of territorial behavior that social anthropologists have suggested), whereas women who are accustomed to smaller personal space may not find the cramped conditions as out of the ordinary. Yet over a longer period of time, these initial reactions may change, particularly when some problem-solving activity needs to be done. As we have seen earlier, men in single-sexed groups tend to be more instrumental while women tend to be more expressive, and in this particular problem-solving situation the instrumental tactics might be more adaptive. Perhaps the propensity of men to be more instrumental, when combined with the greater closeness of the high-density situation, actually results in a more positive, cohesive experience. For women, in contrast, the incompatibility of socioemotional tactics with the problem-solving requirement may be irritated by the extreme closeness and result in more negative reactions. If this explanation is correct, then we could expect to find reversals when the task requirements change. A greater stress on emotional skills should decrease displeasure among women while increasing the antagonism of men. Such investigations need to be done if we are to increase our understanding of women, of men, and of human ecology in general.

WHO IS THE LEADER?

Thus far, we have talked of groups as a collection of individuals each contributing equally to the group outcomes. Yet most groups have some sort of leader, who takes the greatest responsibility for directing the activities of the group members toward their common goal. In many cases, this person may be an *emergent* leader, gradually assuming his or her place with consensus of the group. In other cases, the leader may be *appointed*—by the board of trustees in a university, by the chairperson of the board in an organization, or by the experimenter in a laboratory study.

Looking around at the leaders in the society, we find that most often they are men. While Indira Gandhi and Golda Meir are notable exceptions in the political sphere, they are indeed exceptions.

Women represent more than 20% of labor-union membership but hold less than 5% of the leadership positions.[12] Research has shown that the foreman of a jury panel, selected by fellow jurors, is almost always male (and generally an upper-middle-class white male, at that). Some would argue that the predominance of males in leadership positions reflects the natural order of things. Lionel Tiger, for example, believes that women leaders cannot invoke trust or confidence. He argues that there is an instinctive response toward a man, particularly in times of stress, which would not trigger for a female leader. Others would argue that women can be good leaders but simply have not been given the opportunity or the training to exercise their leadership skills.

At least two questions are important to ask with respect to the roles of men and women as leaders. First, are women as likely as men to emerge as leaders in a group? And second, if a woman is appointed as the leader of a group, what happens? Can she lead as well as a man, and will people follow her as readily as they would a man?

While social psychology has not provided us with an abundance of research on these questions (having tended to focus primarily on male leadership, perhaps reflecting the proportionality of the real world), there are a few recent studies that give us some basis for comparing men and women as leaders.

Our first question asked whether men and women are equally likely to emerge as leaders. Looking at the leaders in the real world, we might immediately suspect that the answer to that question is no. Most research would support that answer. In part, of course, the emergent leader will depend on the characteristics of the group. In an all-female group, for example, it is inevitable that some woman will emerge as the leader. When the group contains both sexes, however, the odds are strongly in favor of a man becoming the leader. In a simplified but elegant demonstration of this event, psychologist Edwin Megargee paired two people in a situation in which the pair had to decide who would be leader and who would be follower.[13] The pairing was not random, however. Based on scores the people had received on a paper-and-pencil measure of dominance, Megargee arranged for each pair to consist of one person who had scored high on a measure of dominance and one person who had scored low. Thus, to the extent that the personality trait measured by the pencil-and-paper test was valid, we would expect that the person who had scored high in dominance would become the leader, while the person low in dominance would be the follower. However, Megargee complicated the situation by varying the sex of the partners. In two of his conditions, both partners were of the same sex (either both male or both female), and they differed in dominance scores as described above. There were few surprises among these subjects. Approximately 70% of the time, the person who scored high in dominance was the person who became the leader of the partnership, and the person who scored low became the follower. In a third case, Megargee paired a high-dominant male with a low-dominant female. Again, the results were as expected. Consistent with what would be expected from the personality scores as well as what might be considered "natural" for a male and female working together, the man became the leader in 90% of the groups. The fourth condition in this study was probably the most interesting. In this case, a woman who scored high in dominance was paired with a man who had scored low in dominance. Here the personality measures conflicted with the normative sex-role behaviors, and the results of the study show that the norms won out. In only 20% of the pairs did the woman become the leader. Perhaps even more interesting are the discussions that preceded the pair's deciding who should be the leader. In the majority of cases, it was the high-dominant woman who made the decision—deciding that her male partner should be the leader.

Thus, at both the political and the laboratory level, it seems clear that a woman is less likely to emerge as the leader, and there is a strong suggestion that women themselves choose not to emerge. But what of women who do, unlike the majority of their peers, attain a leadership position? Are they able to command the respect of their followers? Research conducted within organizational settings points to the existence of negative attitudes toward women managers, but the scarcity of women in management positions has precluded any significant studies of the actual behavior toward women or the relationship between the sex of the manager and measures of productivity.[14] However, within the more arbitrary world of the social-psychology laboratory, it is possible to look at what happens when a woman or man is appointed to be the leader, if only of a short-term experimental group.

Marsha Jacobson and Joan Effertz formed a series of three-person groups, varying both the sex of the leader and the sex of the followers.[15] When the three college-student subjects came to the laboratory for their experiment, they were told they would be participating in a group problem-solving task, and that one person's name would be drawn out of a hat to be the leader. These drawings were rigged so that four different types of groups could be set up. In two cases, all three people in the group were of the same sex (either male or female) and one of the names was drawn at random. In the other two cases, the name drawn to be leader was of one sex while the other two members were of the opposite sex. Thus, a woman was asked to be leader with two men in the group, or a man was appointed leader when the other two group members were women. The problem that the group was asked to solve involved arranging dominoes according to a provided pattern. Only the leader had access to the pattern, and verbal instructions had to be used to instruct the other members. By design, however, the task was so difficult that no group could fully solve it, and thus each group experienced failure under the leadership of the selected student. Jacobson and Effertz were interested in how this experience of failure would affect the leader's perceptions and the followers' perceptions and whether these views would differ with the sex of each person involved.

Did the groups differ in their reactions? First of all, we should mention that each group performed equally well—or equally poorly, since none of the groups was able to complete the task. Yet although the objective performance of each group was the same, the members differed in their evaluations of the group's performance. In both cases where a man was the leader, the other two members of the group rated his performance as significantly worse than when a woman was the leader. It didn't matter which sex the followers were—both men and women rated the male leader less favorably. Ratings of the followers' performance by the leaders showed exactly the opposite pattern: male followers were seen as having done much better than female followers, and again the sex of the leader made no difference in these judgments.

At first glance these results may seem surprising and even opposite from what might be expected. The important key, however, is in remembering that the group failed. If we can assume that men are supposed to be good leaders and women are supposed to be good followers, then we can ask what happens when the group is ineffective. Either the leader didn't lead well, or the followers didn't follow well. If we push this line of argument just a bit further, we might suggest that people would be rated most negatively when they didn't fulfill their role expectations. Thus, men who were expected to be good leaders were doubly cursed when the group didn't succeed. Similarly, women who were supposed to follow well were more negatively evaluated for their performance than men, who might not be expected to be good followers. Of course, to fully support this line of reasoning, we would have to conduct a parallel experiment in which the groups were successful. Under these conditions, the previous reasoning would predict that successful male leaders would be rated more favorably than successful female leaders, and successful female followers would be rated more favorably than successful male followers. Such results would be consistent with the performance judgments we found in Chapter 3, where men were rated more positively for a good performance and more negatively for a poor performance. On the other hand, some of those earlier results also suggest that, if an authority figure commended the woman leader for her strong performance, she might get bonus points for doing better than expected in the leadership role.

We have covered a lot of ground in this chapter: who joins groups, what happens when groups of men and women are in close contact, and how leaders act and are reacted to. Many of these group behaviors can be related to previously discussed patterns of women and men. Stereotypes of males' and females' performance become impressions of leadership. Communication styles are evidenced in the group interaction. Considerations of personal space play a role in the reactions of men and women to high density. Beyond these commonalities, there are factors such as density and leadership behavior that are unique to the group. Unlike Lionel Tiger, we cannot assume that the differences can be explained by a simple principle of "male bonding." Rather, we must continue to look for specific conditions and situations that either minimize or maximize the differences between women and men.

Chapter 11

Men and Women Together: The Basis of Attraction

On the whole, women tend to love men for their character, while men tend to love women for their appearance.

Bertrand Russell

Being a woman is a terribly difficult task, since it consists principally in dealing with men.

Joseph Conrad

The women and men of the previous chapters have proved to be highly complex beings, often showing sharp differences in their goals, their strategies, and their styles of interaction. Yet despite these differences, men and women do get together. Some would argue that the successful relationship between a man and a woman relies on just these differences, with the couple providing a balance of skills. Other observers would say that male-female relationships can't be secure unless both partners develop a broader range of alternatives. Many debates on the future of sex roles focus on just these issues, viewing the state of marriage and families with either apprehension or hope. In this chapter, we'll look at the attraction between men and women and the methods the sexes use to deal with their similarities and differences.[1]

THE ONE WHO IS MY IDEAL

What do women and men seek in a partner? Is the ideal for every man a Miss America? Is the ideal for every woman a Mr. America? Or are the ideals a Betty Crocker and a Henry Ford? There certainly is no shortage of opinion on the matter. Until very recently, a prominent stockbrokerage had its own set of criteria for what men should want in a woman. A test that was required for all persons wishing to be account executives asked the applicants to indicate which qualities in a woman are most important. Putting aside for the moment the problems a woman might have in answering this question, consider the provided choice of answers: dependency, affection, beauty, intelligence, and independence. The would-be executive received maximum points if the chosen response was affection or dependency, partial points if beauty was selected, and a flat zero for picking intelligence or independence.[2] One wonders what the aspiring female account executive would be expected to prefer in a man.

Social psychologists have attempted to answer the question of what men and women view as the ideal by inquiry, rather than by fiat. Many investigators have asked young men and women what characteristics they prefer in the opposite sex, and the results of these studies echo Bertrand Russell's observation. In one such investigation conducted in the mid-1960s, Robert Coombs and William Kenkel coordinated their scientific curiosity with a campus-wide computer dance, in which 500 males and 500 females were matched on the basis of information they filled out on a computer card.[3] In addition to describing themselves, the students were asked to indicate what qualities they would desire in their date. As it turned out, these men and women tended to look for different things in a dating partner. For the men, it was far more important that their date be attractive than it was for a woman. On all other qualities that Coombs and Kenkel included in their questionnaire, however, it was the women who had the more stringent demands. For women, it was more important that their dates have high scholastic ability, be a "big man on campus," wear stylish clothes, dance well, and be of the same race and religion as themselves. These qualities were not always unimportant to men when describing their ideal date, but they were considerably less important to the men than to the women. Russell's observations seem to be right: women are to be loved for their looks and men for their character and values. Other studies have found similar evidence that physical attractiveness is more important to the man in describing his heroine than it is to the woman in picking her hero. Interestingly enough, it is not certain that men actually do respond more strongly to their date's attractiveness than do women. In some cases, it has been reported that women are more influenced by the good looks of a date than men; other studies have shown that physical attractiveness is indeed more important to men.[4] Thus, the reality of the behavior is not as clear as the preferences, but in terms of stated preferences, men show more concern about the physical attractiveness of their date.

In addition to the characteristics of beauty and accomplishments, psychologists have also asked young men and women to indicate what kinds of personality characteristics they prefer a date to have. James Curran, for example, has found that college women describe their ideal date as high on assertiveness and dominance, while for men the ideal woman is higher on dependency. In this case, the ideal carried over to the reality. After an initial date, men reported being more attracted to a woman who had scored low on dominance, while women expressed more attraction for a high-dominant man.[5]

In summary, men and women do express different preferences for the ideal mate. Closely reflecting the stereotypes we saw in Chapter 2, these ideals require attractiveness and submission in the woman and accomplishment and assertiveness in the man. Yet while the stated desires are expressed clearly, there is less evidence that these qualities are crucial when men and women actually get together. Other characteristics come into play in the relationship between a woman and a man.

I'D LIKE YOU TO BE LIKE ME

Although men, and to a lesser extent women, indicate that a partner who is highly attractive is the most desirable, other evidence suggests that both men and women will insert a bit of subjective reality into their actual dating choices. While many may wish their partner to be the most attractive creature on earth, there is, after all, a limit on the number of people that any society considers highly attractive. And if I myself am low on the attractiveness dimension, is it reasonable for me to aspire to the most handsome man in town? Perhaps a more rational strategy would be a preference for someone who is roughly equivalent in physical attractiveness. This "matching hypothesis" has been tested in a number of settings. Although the idea itself seems quite reasonable, earlier studies found little evidence for its validity. For example, when students at the University of Minnesota were paired with dates at a computer dance, the evidence indicated that nearly all the students were most satisfied when their dates were highly attractive. However, later research has revived the matching hypothesis. The critical factor seems to be the possibility of rejection that is involved. When the date is already set up, with little chance for a cancellation, both men and women prefer a more attractive date, no matter how attractive they themselves are. On the other hand, when the date is only tentative or must be arranged, men and women are more inclined to consider their own attractiveness vis-à-vis their prospective date.[6]

In the same way that people prefer a date who is similar in physical attractiveness, they also prefer others who share similar attitudes and values. Although the theoretical interpretations of this relationship between similarity and attraction may vary, few would doubt that it holds true in a wide variety of situations.[7] The majority of studies of similarity and attraction have considered two persons of the same sex. Yet additional studies indicate that we also like persons of the opposite sex who have attitudes similar to our own.[8]

Within this general relationship, however, there is evidence that different types of attitudes may vary in importance for men and women. John Touhey presented male and female students with descriptions of opposite-sex students who were either similar or dissimilar on (a) attitudes toward religion or (b) attitudes toward traditional sexual standards.[9] Touhey found that the man's feelings about the female stranger were most affected by sexual values, with men liking those women who shared their own attitudes about sex more than those who had similar attitudes toward religion. Women, in contrast, were more influenced by the religious attitudes of the man they were evaluating, finding him more attractive if he shared religious values than if he had similar sexual values and viewing him as less likable if he had dissimilar religious values than if he had dissimilar sexual values. The difference in the importance of these two issues takes us back to the Coombs and Kenkel computer date study, where women said that religion was a more important criterion for them and men said it was less important. Men may also be acting consistently with their stated ideals, if we consider sexual attitudes to be related to an expressed interest in physical attractiveness. Yet it is not attractiveness or religiosity per se that is important but rather the similarity in the values of the two partners. Other attitudes and values may also have different amounts of importance for men and women. For any particular couple, we would have to know the importance they placed on these values before we could predict whether similars would attract.

GETTING TO KNOW YOU

Thus far, we have been concerned with the characteristics that men and women see as ideal, or at least attractive, in a person of the opposite sex. While a laboratory experiment may provide us with all this information in advance—what the person looks like, what his or her attitudes are, and so on—in real life we must discover this information through some kind of interchange with the other person.

How do we get to know people of the other sex? What determines whether a glance across a crowded room will be followed by some conversation at closer range? These questions have not been studied much in the social-psychological laboratory, but they are terribly intriguing questions for those interested in how men and women relate. Although the man has traditionally been the one to make the initial approach, at least in the formal sense of asking for a date, it is far from certain that the initial interchange is a one-way street. In fact, one recent study has suggested that the woman is actually the gatekeeper in an initial contact between a man and a woman.

Using a very simple situation, Mark Cary observed how conversations begin when one person enters a room where another person is already sitting.[10] The results were clearest when a woman was sitting in the room and a man entered. First, the two people looked at each other. Then, *if* the woman looked a second time, a conversation would follow. If she didn't look a second time, silence was the rule. To some extent, this pattern is determined by who is in the room first: that person seems to have a slight advantage in signaling the opening for a conversation. However, Cary's results also show that the woman has more power as a gatekeeper. Perhaps you could try this out for yourself at your next party or at your favorite bar and see if the woman indeed controls the beginnings of conversations. The idea is an intriguing one, because it suggests that the relations between men and women are more complex than some people think. Although many suggest that in present times women should be able to ask men out just as easily as men ask women, the fact may be that women have had a good deal of control all along.

No matter who controls the first meeting, getting to know someone obviously requires more than a glance. What happens when a man and a woman begin a conversation? Are there other types of verbal and nonverbal communication that influence the course of the conversation? Chris Kleinke and his colleagues have done some interesting work that shows what happens when a man and woman first meet and talk for 10 or 15 minutes. In one set of experiments, he considered what happens when one person calls the other person by his or her first name.[11] Does that make for a better or worse relationship? Many salespeople consider it a positive tool, and most of us have probably experienced the ingratiating type who constantly uses our first name as he or she tries to convince us to buy some product. However, most people react negatively to such usage when an ulterior motive can be spotted. The job applicant who continually calls the interviewer by name is generally viewed as being insincere. What happens when ulterior motives are not so obvious, such as when a man and a woman are simply talking to each other? Kleinke's results suggest that men and women respond differently to the tactic. In one such study, two men were interviewed at the same time by an attractive female student. The interviewer treated each of the two men in the same way with one exception: she called one of the men by his first name 11 times during the interview while not referring to the other man by name at all. At the conclusion of these interviews, the man whose name had been used was convinced that the interviewer had liked him more than the other student. Similarly, the student whose name had not been used felt that he was liked less than was his companion. The same pattern was found in the men's ratings of the interviewer. The man whose name had been used liked the interviewer more than did the man who had not been called by name. In a second study, the tables were turned. In this instance, a man and a woman were put together for 15 minutes and simply instructed to get to know each other. However, the man was previously told by the experimenter either to use the woman's name as often as possible or not to use her name at all. At the end of these conversations, the woman liked a man who had not used her name more than one who had (on the average, the man used the woman's name six times during the course of the 15-minute conversation). Not only did she think the name-user was more of a phony, simply trying to make a good impression, but she was also less enthusiastic about talking to him in a later conversation. While these studies suggest that men and women react differently to name-usage, we can't really be certain, because the two studies were not identical. Two men vying for one woman may be quite different from a one-to-one situation. To know for certain, we would have to conduct two more experiments that parallel the previous two.

In another look at what happens when men and women get together, Chris Kleinke asked subjects to talk about anything they wanted for ten minutes. [12] At the end of ten minutes, he gave the two students false information about either how much they had looked at the other person during the conversation or how much the other person had looked at them. In some cases, the experimenter told one person that he or she had looked at the other person much more than is typical in such a setting. In other cases, the person was told that his or her gazing was average or below the average for the situation. Again, men and women responded differently to this information. When the woman thought that her male partner had gazed at her a lot, she found him the least attractive. In contrast, the men rated their female partner as least attractive and interesting when they believed she had not looked at them very much. It is interesting to consider these results in the light of our earlier discussion of nonverbal behavior. Recall that women in general make more eye contact than do men. Perhaps because we either consciously or unconsciously are aware of this norm, our reactions to discrepant behavior are stronger. Women are expected to engage in more eye contact, and thus, when the woman does not, her male partner views her as less attractive. On the other hand, if we assume that men will not make much eye contact, then the man who does may be viewed as less attractive, perhaps guilty of harboring some ulterior motives.

Getting to know one another seems to be a very complicated process, and it may seem a wonder that men and women ever get together. Of course much of this interchange is probably quite unconscious. We look, or begin to talk, or use someone's name, often without giving the matter any serious thought. And this is probably as it should be. Nevertheless, it is fascinating to look more closely at how men and women do typically act in these situations, and how they exert different patterns of control that perpetuate or terminate the relationship.

FROM THIS MOMENT ON

Once the initial contact is made, and some interest is indicated on both sides, men and women often go on to date, fall in love, and live together and/or marry. Until recently, social psychologists gave relatively little attention to these matters, choosing instead to focus on initial impressions. In part, this choice was undoubtedly a pragmatic decision: it is certainly far easier to study first impressions in the laboratory than to study long-term romances outside the confines of the lab. In the past few years, however, some social psychologists have begun to tackle this larger problem. Joining philosophers, poets, and sages from centuries back, the social psychologist has begun to ask "What is love?"

It has often been assumed that women are the more romantic of the two sexes, more prone to be swept off their feet and fall madly in love with a less emotional, less romantic man. Yet the available evidence does not support this belief. In the early study by Coombs and Kenkel, for example, in which couples were paired for a dance on the basis of computer cards, women showed themselves to be decidedly less impressed.[13] When asked how much romantic attraction they felt for their date, 52% of the women but only 38% of the men replied "Absolutely no romantic attraction at all." Similarly, 19% of the men but only 7% of the women reported strong attraction for their computer-picked date. The same kinds of results were found when the students were asked the likelihood that they could be happily married to someone like their date. Fifty percent of the men but only 39% of the women felt that was possible. Perhaps because women were more demanding in their initial preferences, they were less satisfied with the outcome. Of course, we could suggest that women really are the more romantic sex, at least in idealistic terms, but that reality always falls far short of their ideals.

Yet even in the realm of ideals, women are less romantic than men. Zick Rubin asked 200 dating couples at the University of Michigan how much each agreed with a number of statements reflecting romantic love. [14] Examples of some of these statements include "A person should marry whomever he loves regardless of social position" and "Economic security should be carefully considered before selecting a marriage partner." Men, as compared with women, were substantially more likely to agree with the first statement and to disagree with the second.

Thus, women do not seem to be the more romantic of the sexes. Indeed, they turn out to be rather pragmatic about marriage, assessing factors such as economic and social status before they fall madly in love. Apart from ideals, how do men and women feel about a relationship once it has been established? Again, Zick Rubin can provide some answers. During the course of his research, Rubin has developed two additional scales: one to measure love and one to measure liking. The love scale was designed to tap the components of attachment, caring, and intimacy. Examples of questions from this scale include "I would do almost anything for _____" and "I would forgive _____ for practically anything." Rubin's liking scale is more geared toward the respect we have for another person, regardless of whether we're romantically involved. Questions on this scale refer to the perceived judgment and maturity of another person, for example, and to their likability.

When we ask partners in a dating relationship to complete these questionnaires, we find that men and women love their mate equally well. On the liking scale, however, women indicate that they like their men more than men like their women. This latter finding is not a total surprise, if we recall the stereotype findings of Chapter 2. Rubin's liking scale contains many of the characteristics that the society judges to be more typical of men, and these dating partners seem to share the same conceptions despite the intimacy of their relationship. Love is indeed complex: men have higher romantic ideals, men and women love equally much, but women like their partners more.

The development of a relationship from acquaintance to dating to marriage (or some other form of permanent relationship) has also been a topic of interest to social scientists. Some theorists have proposed a sequence of stages in the mate-selection process that contribute to the outcome. In this model developed by Alan Kerckhoff and Keith Davis,[15] proximity is the first filter: people who are likely to encounter each other are more likely to get together than those who are not. At a second stage, a relationship is affected by similarity in attitudes and values. Some of these attitudes have been discussed earlier; others include family values such as economic security and healthy and happy children. Kerckhoff and Davis found that dating couples who showed high agreement on the relative importance of these values were more likely to move toward a permanent relationship than those couples who showed little agreement. At a later stage in the relationship, these authors suggest that complementarity of needs is important.

Complementarity in its simplest form means "opposites attract," and the idea has had a long history in the study of relationships. Carl Jung was an early proponent of the notion; sociologist Robert Winch was responsible for its development within the literature of romance.[16] The crux of the complementarity argument is that people who differ on certain needs and personality characteristics can offer each other valuable sources of reinforcement. For example, if Jane is a dominant type of person, it may be most satisfying for her to pair up with someone who likes to be dominated. That way both Jane and her mate can satisfy each other's needs, the one to dominate and the other to be dominated. While this notion seems a reasonable one and has received some support,[17] other studies have failed to confirm the importance of complementarity in long-term relationships.[18] One problem is in identifying which personality characteristics work this way and how broad their influence is. Possibly there are only one or two personality dimensions for which complementarity is an important consideration. In this regard, it is perhaps not surprising that dominance versus submissiveness is an easy and often-used example but that it is difficult to think of many others. It seems less likely, for example, that an extrovert would be happy with a totally introverted person or that a trusting person would enjoy the company of a highly suspicious soul. Thus, the status of complementarity must remain with a question mark.

A similar kind of balance has been proposed to exist in the husband-wife relationship. Sociologist Talcott Parsons was an early advocate of the view that the marriage state represents a balance between instrumental and expressive roles, such as those we discussed in the previous chapter.[19] According to his view, husbands exert the instrumental roles in a family while wives fulfill the expressive functions. Although this idea of complementarity has appeal for many, the research again is not so cooperative. A number of studies have shown that in a marriage relationship both partners fulfill both roles. [20]

I suspect that patterns that develop in a permanent relationship are far more complex than investigators have yet acknowledged. These relationships provide a rich background for investigators of male and female behavior and the situations affecting that behavior. We have seen that the interactions between men and women encompass and sometimes modify many of the behavior patterns that are characteristic of male and female strangers. Styles of communication, strategies of interaction, and stereotyped views all contribute to the relationship between a woman and a man. Consequently, any changes in these more general patterns will undoubtedly alter the more personal relationships as well. Changes in stereotypes may affect measures of respect. A greater range of communication styles could affect the division of roles within the partnership. The important point is that men and women together cannot be separate from men and women apart. Understanding one requires a knowledge of the other.

Chapter 12

Women, Men, and Androgyns

Everyone is partly man and partly woman.

Virginia Woolf

The truth is, a great mind must be androgynous.

Samuel Coleridge

In the preceding chapters, we have looked at how men and women act and interact in a variety of situations. In considering the similarities and differences in behavior, we have divided human beings into two categories—men and women. Biologically, this division certainly makes sense, and as we look around us it is usually quite simple to make the same categorization. Furthermore, because it is so easy to distinguish females from males, one can argue that men and women tend to have different sets of experiences as they grow up, which result in different patterns of behavior in later life. The evidence of the previous chapters would support the argument that men and women, by their nature or by their experience, do (on the average) react differently to many situations.

Yet many people would argue that this kind of split is an artificial one. While women and men may be visibly different, they are not necessarily different in a psychological sense. Depending on particular socialization experiences, some men may be very feminine in their interests and behaviors, and some women may be very masculine. Does it make more sense to look at the masculinity or femininity of people rather than their biological sex? Let's look at the evidence.

MEASURING MASCULINITY AND FEMININITY

In the most general sense, masculinity and femininity are considered to be relatively stable traits of the individual, rooted in anatomy, physiology, and early experience.[1] Furthermore, it is assumed that, although there will be a certain number of exceptions, most biological males will be high in psychological masculinity, and most biological females will be high in psychological femininity.

These assumptions are very clearly rooted in the development of questionnaires designed to measure masculinity and femininity. Masculinity is what men typically do, and femininity is what women typically do.

To understand this operation more clearly, let's consider how the typical masculinity-femininity (M-F) scale is designed. The test constructor starts with a large number of questions that cover a variety of areas: interests, activities, personality characteristics, and values. Then a group of men and women are asked to respond to the various questions. Once these data are collected, the investigator looks carefully at those questions that men and women answer differently. If men endorse an item more often than women, then that item is considered to represent masculinity. Similarly, if women agree with a particular item more frequently than do men, that item is considered to be an indication of femininity. A final M-F measure is then constructed based on the items that showed differences between men and women.

You might suspect that this method leads to some circularity, and indeed it does. Masculine and feminine are simply what men and women do, so we're really not very far ahead of where we were in considering men and women as biological entities. However, some men will score high on femininity on such tests, and some women will score high on masculinity, so the correspondence is not perfect. Perhaps these psychological concepts may yet prove more meaningful.

However, there is another problem with the method of forming M-F scales. Consider the investigator who assesses the attitudes of the people in a particular culture and finds that men prefer a shower to a bath, while for women the preferences are reversed. Using the typical method of constructing M-F scales, our investigator would include this item as an index of masculinity or femininity. But what if our investigator is a curious sort and returns to the same culture 20 years later, only to find that the preferences of men and women have changed? Now women say they prefer showers, while men claim that baths are better. The result would be a change in the scoring of the M-F scale. Now bath lovers would be more masculine, and those who preferred showers would be considered feminine. We begin to see that this trait of masculinity and femininity is not terribly stable and enduring after all. Yet before we become too cynical, we should look more carefully at what measurements of masculinity and femininity have shown.

Research has shown that a person's masculinity or femininity score can be affected by a number of demographic variables. For example, a number of studies have shown that, as a person's level of education increases, the average M-F score changes as well.[2] The highly educated man is more feminine than his less-educated counterpart, and as women increase in education level, they become more masculine on the standard M-F scale. Other studies have found differences in masculinity and femininity associated with age, suggesting that men become more feminine in their interests and traits as they grow older. Even geographical location has been found to be related to the average masculinity and femininity scores of the people in those areas.[3]

Surprisingly little work has been done, however, that would demonstrate the connection between a person's M-F score and other forms of behavior. Some researchers have shown that M-F scores are related to a person's creativity,[4] while others have shown that people will learn material more readily if it is consistent with their psychological masculinity or femininity.[5] Yet in most of those areas we have considered in this book—behaviors such as altruism, aggression, competition, and nonverbal communication styles—we know very little about the relationship between masculinity and femininity and behavior. We might predict that we would find masculine people acting very much like males and feminine people acting very much like females, but there just isn't much evidence to support the predictions.

Although this lack of evidence is not particularly comforting, there is an even more serious problem with the traditional measures of masculinity and femininity. In nearly every scale that has been developed over the past several decades, test constructors have assumed that masculinity and femininity represent the opposite ends of a single dimension. In other words, if a particular characteristic is not masculine, then it must be feminine. This assumption is reflected in most of the M-F scales that have been developed. Generally, people are given a choice between two responses. Selecting one of these responses will result in a point scored for masculinity, while the choice of the other response will add a point to the femininity score. The fewer masculine items a person agrees with, the more feminine that person is considered, and vice versa.

Recently, psychologists have begun to question these assumptions. Is it reasonable to assume that masculinity and femininity represent a single dimension? Does a person have to be either masculine *or* feminine? Or can a person be both masculine and feminine, combining characteristics of both sexes in a single person? Phrased in another way, is it possible for people to be androgynous?

THE DEVELOPMENT OF ANDROGYNY

Biologists have known for years that men and women possess quantities of both male and female hormones. The balance between the hormones is different for men and women, but both kinds are present in the male and in the female body. Perhaps psychologically there can be a parallel coexistence. Writers for centuries have suggested that such a coexistence is possible. Plato, in presenting a myth of sexuality in the *Symposium,* described beings who were half male and half female. Many years later, Samuel Coleridge asserted that the great mind is an androgynous mind, combining both masculine and feminine traits. More recently, Carolyn Heilbrun has argued that the concept of androgyny can be found in major literary works throughout the centuries, and she buttresses her arguments with quotes from Aristophanes through Shakespeare to Virginia Woolf.[6]

Within the field of psychology, Sandra Bem deserves the major credit for directing the attention of investigators to the concept of androgyny.[7] People, she suggests, are not as limited as the earlier conceptions of masculinity and femininity would suggest. According to this early research, the world is made up of masculine males, feminine females, and sex-reversed deviants. Bem, along with a growing number of other investigators,[8] believes that androgyny is a meaningful concept. Men and women may have both masculine and feminine characteristics. A person may be both assertive and yielding, both instrumental and expressive. While the earlier methods of measuring masculinity and femininity could not uncover this type of person, Bem believes that androgyns are alive and well in 20th-century life.

To measure androgyny, Bem constructed two separate scales— one that measures masculine characteristics and one that measures feminine characteristics.[9] Each scale consists of 20 personality characteristics that are considered desirable in our culture. The masculinity scale contains, for example, such items as "competitive," "self-reliant," and "analytical." On the femininity scale are items like "affectionate," "sensitive to the needs of others," and "yielding." Bem's first important finding was that these two scales are independent of one another. Earlier investigators had assumed that a person who is high on masculinity will necessarily be low on femininity, and they constructed their questionnaires in such a way that their assumption was automatically true. Because Bem used two separate scales, however, she was able to test the assumption that masculinity and femininity are the mirror image of each other. Her results showed that they are not. In statistical terms, the correlation between the two scales approximated zero. What this means is that a person who scores high on femininity may be high, medium, or low on masculinity, and vice versa. Knowing a person's score on one scale gives you no ability to predict that person's score on the other scale.

Androgyny, as defined by Bem, is reflected in the balance between a person's score on these two scales. If a person's scores on the two scales are relatively equal, then that person is considered androgynous. Both masculine and feminine characteristics are endorsed in approximately equal proportions. For example, an androgynous person might say that he or she was competitive, independent, and athletic but also loyal, shy, and understanding. Such a self-description would tend to indicate a balance between masculine and feminine characteristics. Other individuals might show a much greater difference in their endorsement of items on the masculinity and femininity scales. A person who agreed with a large number of items on the masculinity scale but who felt very few items on the femininity scale were accurate self-descriptions would be considered masculine sex-typed. A feminine sex-typed person would be one who agreed with many of the items on the femininity scale and very few on the masculinity scale. In her initial work, Bem found that approximately 50% of the California college students that she tested could be considered traditionally sex-typed feminine females or masculine males. More than a third of the people in her sample, however, were androgynous—showing a relatively equal balance between masculine and feminine traits. The remainder of her sample were considered sex-reversed—women who scored much higher on the masculinity scale than on the femininity scale and men who scored higher on femininity than on masculinity.

Accepting Bem's notion of masculinity and femininity as two separate dimensions, University of Texas psychologists Janet Spence, Robert Helmreich, and Joy Stapp have advocated an alternative conception of androgyny.[10] These investigators argue that, while masculinity and femininity represent two separate sets of characteristics, a simple balance between these characteristics does not guarantee androgyny. For example, someone who felt he or she had few masculine characteristics and also had few feminine characteristics would be androgynous by Bem's definition, in that there would be a balance between the two sets of traits. In contrast, Spence and her colleagues would argue that only those persons who had a high percentage of both masculine and feminine traits would be truly androgynous. Theoretically, this latter conception is surely closer to the ideas of Plato, Coleridge, and Heilbrun, pointing to a person who has developed skills in both arenas rather than withdrawing from both.[11] We'll return to this distinction, but let's first consider the relevance of androgyny for behavior.

WHY ANDROGYNY?

It is certainly of some interest to know that masculinity and femininity are independent of one another: that both men and women can have either masculine or feminine characteristics or have both at the same time. Probably the more interesting question, however, is what are androgynous people like? Are there advantages to being androgynous as opposed to being more traditionally sex-typed? Sandra Bem leaves no doubt about her opinion; she considers androgyny the more positive state. In support of her contention, she has reviewed much of the earlier literature on sex-typing and finds considerable evidence to suggest that strong sex-typing may not be the best state of affairs. For example, a review of the literature shows that boys and girls who show stronger cross-sex typing (boys with some feminine traits and girls with some masculine traits) are generally higher in intelligence and show more creativity.[12] Some other evidence reviewed by Bem suggests that highly sex-typed girls express more anxiety and show lower psychological adjustment. Results for boys are not as clear, but at the least they do not give strong evidence that sex-typing is best.[13]

An even stronger case for the value of both masculine and feminine traits has recently been presented by Spence, Helmreich, and Stapp.[14] These investigators looked at the relationship between sex-role identification and self-esteem and found that for both men and women high scores on both the masculine and the feminine items were associated with high self-esteem. In contrast, those people who indicated a low proportion of both masculine and feminine traits were characterized by low self-esteem, supporting the view of these investigators that an even balance is not enough. Traditionally sex-typed persons, in comparison, were midway between these two groups in terms of self-esteem. Spence and her colleagues also report that individuals high on both masculine and feminine characteristics may have different backgrounds from more sex-typed individuals. For example, they have found that androgyns received more honors and awards during their school years, dated more, and were sick less often than were sex-typed individuals.[15]

Beyond these differences in background and self-esteem, Sandra Bem has suggested that the androgynous person may be capable of functioning effectively in a wider variety of situations than the sex-typed individual can. For example, in a situation in which assertiveness and independence are required, a masculine sex-typed person should be more effective than a feminine sex-typed person. However, if Bem's theorizing is true, the androgynous male or female should be able to function just as effectively in such a situation as the masculine person. In a similar manner, we would expect that, in a situation calling for warmth and emotional expressiveness, feminine persons would be more effective than masculine persons. Again, Bem would predict that the androgynous person would also be able to do well in this situation. Thus, Bem would argue that the androgynous person has a wider range of capabilities. Depending on what the situation requires, the androgynous person can show masculine assertiveness or feminine warmth and should be equally effective in both situations. The sex-typed person, in contrast, is more restricted, being limited to doing well only in those situations where the requirements are consistent with the person's own sex-typed characteristics.

In her first test of these theoretical predictions, Bem set up two different situations that presumably had different kinds of requirements.[16] The first situation was a typical conformity experiment. Subjects in this experiment were told that they were participating in a study of humor. Each student was asked to look at a series of cartoons and rate each cartoon for its funniness. However, before giving his or her own rating, each student heard two other subjects give their opinions of the cartoon's humor. Relying on the early studies that showed greater female conformity (though, as we saw in Chapter 10, these findings are not wholly consistent), Bem predicted that in this type of conformity situation, both sex-typed men and androgynous men and women would show less conformity than would sex-typed women. Her predictions proved to be correct. Feminine males and females conformed on an average of 23 out of 36 possible trials, while both masculine subjects and androgynous subjects (males and females) showed less conformity, following the group's opinions on less than half of the total trials.

Bem then applied the same kind of reasoning to a second task, this time one in which women would be expected to be more facile. In this second situation, subjects were given the opportunity to play with a small kitten, and the experimenters recorded how long each subject did this. The expectation was that both feminine sex-typed persons and androgynous persons would play with the kitten longer than would masculine sex-typed persons. Among the men, Bem found some support for her predictions. Feminine and androgynous men did play with the kitten more than did masculine men. For women, however, the results were a bit confusing. The androgynous women played with the kitten quite a bit, but the feminine women did not; in fact, these latter women played with the kitten much less than did masculine women.

In later studies, Sandra Bem and her colleagues have found some evidence that when given a series of choices sex-typed individuals are more likely to select own-sex behaviors and avoid cross-sex behaviors.[17] Yet once again, these findings were much clearer among the men than they were for the women.

Bem's failure so far to find unambiguous support for the connection between androgyny and behavior is certainly not uncommon in the early stages of research. While some of the findings are promising, it is clear that we are only beginning to tap the top of an iceberg that may prove to be much larger (and much more complicated) as the research continues. A more fundamental difficulty may lie in Bem's conception of androgyny. Logically, there is no reason to expect someone who possesses few masculine or feminine traits to behave in either terribly masculine or feminine ways. Such persons may in fact be more neutral in all their behaviors. In contrast, if we adopt a notion of androgyny as representing only those people who are high in both masculinity and femininity, then Bem's predictions about the behavior of androgynous people should hold true.

Androgyny is an exciting concept and deserves much more attention by investigators in the future. Intuitively, it makes a great deal of sense to think that people can combine masculine and feminine traits and be free to use either type according to the situation. As many recent commentators have suggested, it might be good if men could express emotions, disclose their feelings with other people, and worry less about dominating all people in all situations. At the same time, many have argued that women should be able to be more assertive, to strive for achievement in the marketplace, and to be independent enough to avoid total reliance on others. If the early theorizing is true, an androgynous person could be all of these things.

Yet even with this alternative conception, some questions remain. What kinds of predictions could we make, for example, in a situation where either a masculine or feminine response may be appropriate? In many of the social settings we have studied, there is not necessarily a better or worse strategy. Men and women have frequently been found to differ, but the labels of good or bad cannot be so readily applied. What would our androgynous person do in these settings? Androgyny may prove very useful in our understanding of some behavior in some settings. However, the concept may be most useful in conjunction with, rather than as a replacement of, our accumulated knowledge of the behavior of women and men.

Postscript on
the Future

In 1869, the social philosopher John Stuart Mill claimed that it was impossible for him to know the true nature of men and women. He suggested that the existing relationship between the sexes prevented a person from knowing what women and men could be like and presented instead merely a picture of what was true in the conventional society of 19th-century England. Now, over 100 years after Mill's statement, are we any closer to knowing the true nature of men and women?

In the preceding chapters, we have considered the social behavior of women and men in a wide variety of situations. While you must draw your own conclusions, my opinion is that we have made considerable progress in our understanding of the nature of women and men. Seeking the "true nature," however, may be a futile quest. The behavior of women and men can't be separated from their time and place, and the sexes will never develop in a vacuum apart from the pressures of a particular society. Our questions must instead focus on how the potential of women and men will be altered under varying circumstances.

Simplified statements of the "true nature" rest in the province of stereotypes. We have seen that the stereotypes of what men and women are supposedly like persist, suggesting that there are strong and numerous differences between women and men that are apparent in all situations. Not only do these stereotypes exist as abstract concepts in our heads, but they also influence the judgments we make of individual men and women who do not fit our preconceived notions. Frequently, as we have seen, these judgments operate to the disadvantage of the person in question. The high performance of a woman may be explained away by luck, or the low performance of a man may be judged as more devastating than it is. The assertive woman may be labeled extremely aggressive, and the man who discloses personal hopes and fears may be viewed as weak and incompetent. Such stereotyped judgments preserve beliefs in what the nature of women and men really is.

Yet despite the persistence of stereotypes, the studies of social behavior suggest that there are relatively few characteristics in which men and women consistently differ. Men and women both seem to be capable of being aggressive, helpful, and alternately cooperative and competitive. In other words, there is little evidence that the nature of women and men is so inherently different that we are justified in making stereotyped generalizations.

On the other hand, from the social psychologist's view, we've seen that there are many situations in which men and women do act quite differently. We can identify situations in which men are apt to be more aggressive than women and other situations in which women and men will not differ. We can specify the conditions under which women will be more helpful than men and other conditions when the reverse will be true. Apparently the nature of the sexes, in and of itself, is not so very different—in most cases, men and women are capable of exercising the same kinds of behavior. Yet the choices that men and women make in different situations may vary widely, and it is only by considering both the sex and the situation that we can arrive at any real understanding of the nature of men and women. Certainly such an analysis is not as simple as the more stereotyped view that "men are this way" and "women are that way." But truth is not necessarily simple.

What of the nature of women and men in the future? Prediction is always difficult, and even the best clairvoyants have only a moderately successful record. Nonetheless, let me offer a few suggestions based on my interpretation of the evidence. First of all, the fact that men and women do not show many consistent differences—differences that can be observed in any and all situations—suggests that even if biology has some role, its effects are not immutable. The commonality of human behavior is more pronounced than any sex differences, and the role of socialization seems to be primarily channeling this behavior potential into certain arenas. The human being is capable of aggression, love, cooperation, and competition, but the male and female are taught that these behaviors are appropriate under different circumstances. It is not the case, for example, that women are incapable of being aggressive— rather they have learned to display aggression only in certain situations. Similarly, men are not incapable of disclosing things about themselves, but instead they have developed habits that lead them to minimize such behavior.

If the behaviors of men and women are different only in the performance but not in the potential, what does this say about the future of women and men? To me, it says that the possibilities for change are great. To the extent that the society does not define different patterns for men and women, then each sex will be free to develop its complete human potential. Should such changes occur, we would expect to find that men and women would not act so differently. In other words, androgyny is a realistic possibility.

At the same time, we should anticipate that other cultures may reveal differences between men and women that we haven't observed in our own society. If men and women differ not in their capabilities but rather in the occasions when certain behaviors will be shown, then we may well find variations in other cultures. Different ground rules may have been established as to when particular behaviors are appropriate, and different behaviors may have been labeled masculine and feminine as well. While biology has caused men and women to be different, both in appearance and in certain reproductive capabilities, the psychology of women and men is not so different, and it seems to be a result of cultural expectations and values rather than inherent possibilities. As we continue to study the sexes, we'll learn more about the nature of these expectations and the functional value they may serve for a particular culture.

In many ways, we are only at a starting point. Recognizing that the potential of each sex is not so very different, we must direct our questions to the how and the why of particular sex roles that develop. In this search, the future may serve as our laboratory as we watch the behavior of men and women change or stay the same. If changes are great, this book may serve only as a historical document, providing an account of the behavior of men and women in the middle part of the 20th century. On the other hand, as astronomers and geoscientists must deal with changes over centuries, so the social scientist may have to deal with changes over decades. To that end, I hope this book has provided at least one link on the continuum of time.

Footnotes

CHAPTER 1

1. Eleanor Emmons Maccoby and Carol Nagy Jacklin, *The Psychology of Sex Differences* (Stanford, Calif.: Stanford University Press, 1974).
2. Douglas S. Holmes and Bruce W. Jorgensen, "Do Personality and Social Psychologists Study Men More than Women?," *Representative Research in Social Psychology*, 1971, *2*, 71-76.
3. For example, see J.E. Garai and A. Scheinfeld, "Sex Differences in Mental and Behavioral Traits," *Genetic Psychology Monographs*, 1968, *77*, 169-299. Also Lewis M. Terman and Leona E. Tyler, "Psychological Sex Differences," in L. Carmichael (ed.), *A Manual of Child Psychology* (New York: Wiley, 1954), chap. 19.
4. Maccoby and Jacklin, op. cit.
5. Donald M. Broverman, Edward L. Klaiber, Yutaka Kobayashi, and William Vogel, "Roles of Activation and Inhibition in Sex Differences in Cognitive Abilities," *Psychological Review*, 1968, *75*, 23-50.
6. Counterarguments to the Broverman et al. position include Mary B. Parlee, "Comments on 'Roles of Activation and Inhibition in Sex Differences in Cognitive Abilities' by D. M. Broverman, E. L. Klaiber, Y. Kobayashi, and W. Vogel," *Psychological Review*, 1972, *79*, 180-184. A thorough discussion of this issue can also be found in Maccoby and Jacklin, op. cit.
7. For more information on the biological evidence, the following sources are recommended. Frank A. Beach (ed.), *Sex and Behavior* (New York: Wiley, 1965); Corinne Hutt, *Males and Females* (Middlesex, England: Penguin Books, 1972); S. Levine, "Sex Differences in the Brain," *Scientific American*, 1966, *214*, 84-90.
8. Maccoby and Jacklin, op. cit.
9. Maccoby and Jacklin, op. cit.
10. Maccoby and Jacklin, op. cit.
11. Maccoby and Jacklin, op. cit.
12. Walter Mischel, "A Social Learning View of Sex Differences in Behavior," in E. E. Maccoby (ed.), *The Development of Sex Differences* (Stanford, Calif.: Stanford University Press, 1966), pp. 56-81.
13. Leslie Zebrowitz McArthur and Beth Gabrielle Resko, "The Portrayal of

Men and Women in American Television Commercials," *Journal of Social Psychology*, in press.

14.   Women on Words and Images, *Dick and Jane as Victims: Sex Stereotyping in Children's Readers* (Princeton, N.J.: Women on Words and Images, 1972). Also Lenore J. Weitzman, Deborah Eifler, Elizabeth Hokada, and Catherine Ross, "Sex-Role Socialization in Picture Books for Pre-School Children," *American Journal of Sociology*, 1972, 77, 1125-1150.

15.   Herbert Barry III, Margaret K. Bacon, and Irvin L. Child, "A Cross-Cultural Survey of Some Sex Differences in Socialization," *Journal of Abnormal and Social Psychology*, 1957, 55 327-332.

16.   Beatrice Whiting and Carolyn Pope Edwards, "A Cross-Cultural Analysis of Sex Differences in the Behavior of Children Aged Three through Eleven," *Journal of Social Psychology*, 1973, 91, 171-188.

17.   Patricia Draper, "!Kung Women: Contrasts in Sex Egalitarianism in the Foraging and Sedentary Contexts," in R. Reiter (ed.), *Toward an Anthropology of Women* (New York: Monthly Review Press, in press).

CHAPTER 2

1   Caroline T. MacBrayer, "Differences in Perception of the Opposite Sex by Males and Females," *Journal of Social Psychology*, 1960, 52, 309-314.

2.   John P. McKee and Alex C. Sherriffs, "The Differential Evaluation of Males and Females," *Journal of Personality*, 1957, 25, 356-371.

3.   Paul S. Rosenkrantz, Susan R. Vogel, Helen Bee, Inge K. Broverman, and Donald M. Broverman, "Sex-Role Stereotypes and Self-Concepts in College Students," *Journal of Consulting and Clinical Psychology*, 1968, 32, 287-295.

4.   Inge K. Broverman, Donald M. Broverman, Frank E. Clarkson, Paul S. Rosenkrantz, and Susan R. Vogel, "Sex-Role Stereotypes and Clinical Judgments of Mental Health," *Journal of Consulting Psychology*, 1972, 34, 1-7.

5.   Virginia Ellen Schein, "The Relationship between Sex Role Stereotypes and Requisite Management Characteristics," *Journal of Applied Psychology*, 1973, 57, 95-100.

6.   Jeanne Marecek, "When Stereotypes Hurt: Responses to Dependent and Aggressive Communications" (paper presented at Eastern Psychological Association meeting, 1974).

7.   Janet T. Spence, Robert Helmreich, and Joy Stapp, "Likability, Sex-Role Congruence of Interest, and Competence: It All Depends on How You Ask," *Journal of Applied Social Psychology*, in press. Also Janet T. Spence and Robert Helmreich, "Who Likes Competent Women: Competence, Sex-Role Congruence of Interests, and Subjects' Attitudes toward Women as Determinants of Interpersonal Attraction," *Journal of Applied Social Psychology*, 1972, 2, 197-213.

8.   Two recent studies that varied the specific values expressed by unseen women were: B. A. Seyfried and Clyde Hendrick, "When Do Opposites Attract? When They Are Opposite in Sex and Sex-Role Attitudes," *Journal of Personality and Social Psychology*, 1973, 25, 15-20; and David R. Shaffer and Carol Wegley, "Success Orientation and Sex-Role Congru-

ence as Determinants of the Attractiveness of Competent Women," *Journal of Personality*, 1974, *42*, 586-600.

9. Lenore J. Weitzman, Deborah Eifler, Elizabeth Hokada, and Catherine Ross, "Sex Role Socialization in Picture Books for Preschool Children," *American Journal of Sociology*, 1972, *77*, 1125-1150. See also Women on Words and Images, *Dick and Jane as Victims: Sex Stereotyping in Children's Readers* (P.O. Box 2163, Princeton, N.J., 1972).

10. Leslie Zebrowitz McArthur and Beth Gabrielle Resko, "The Portrayal of Men and Women in American Television Commercials," *Journal of Social Psychology*, in press.

11. Gale K. Stolz, Gary Hicks, Sharon Gaik, and John D. Edwards, "The Occupational Roles of Women in Magazines and Books" (unpublished paper, Loyola University, 1974).

12. Irene Hanson Frieze, "Changing Self-Images and Sex-Role Stereotypes in College Women" (paper presented at American Psychological Association meetings, 1974).

13. Virginia E. O'Leary and Charlene E. Depner, "College Males' Ideal Female: Changes in Sex-Role Stereotypes," *Journal of Social Psychology*, 1975, *95*, 139-140.

14. Susan R. Vogel, Inge K. Broverman, Donald M. Broverman, Frank E. Clarkson, and Paul S. Rosenkrantz, "Maternal Employment and Perception of Sex-Roles among College Students," *Developmental Psychology*, 1970, *3*, 384-391.

CHAPTER 3

1. Philip A. Goldberg, "Are Women Prejudiced Against Women?," *Transaction*, April 1968, 28-30.

2. Sandra L. Bem and Daryl J. Bem, "Case Study of a Non-Conscious Ideology: Training the Woman to Know Her Place." In D. J. Bem, *Beliefs, Attitudes, and Human Affairs* (Monterey, Calif.: Brooks/Cole, 1970), pp. 80-99.

3. Harriet Mischel, "Sex Bias in the Evaluation of Professional Achievements," *Journal of Educational Psychology*, 1974, *66*, 157-166.

4. Some of the numerous reports that demonstrate this bias are Robert L. Dipboye, Howard L. Fromkin, and Kent Wiback, "Relative Importance of Applicant Sex, Attractiveness, and Scholastic Standing in Evaluation of Job Applicants," *Journal of Applied Psychology*, 1975, *60*, 39-45; also Linda S. Fidell, "Empirical Verification of Sex Discrimination in Hiring Practices in Psychology," *American Psychologist*, 1970, *25*, 1094-1098.

5. Gail I. Pheterson, Sara B. Kiesler, and Philip A. Goldberg, "Evaluation of the Performance of Women as a Function of their Sex, Achievement, and Personal History," *Journal of Personality and Social Psychology*, 1971, *19*, 114-118.

6. For more complete discussions of equity theory, see J. Stacy Adams, "Inequity in Social Exchange," in L. Berkowitz (ed.), *Advances in Experimental Social Psychology*, vol. 2 (New York: Academic Press, 1965). Also Elaine Walster, Ellen Berscheid, and G. William Walster, "New Directions in Equity Research," *Journal of Personality and Social Psychology*, 1973, *25*, 151-177.

7. Gerald S. Leventhal and James W. Michaels, "Locus of Cause and Equity Motivation as Determinants of Reward Allocation," *Journal of Personality and Social Psychology,* 1971, *17,* 229-235.
8. Janet Taynor and Kay Deaux, "When Women Are More Deserving than Men: Equity, Attribution, and Perceived Sex Differences," *Journal of Personality and Social Psychology,* 1973, *28,* 360-367.
9. Fritz Heider, *The Psychology of Interpersonal Relations* (New York: Wiley, 1958).
10. Kay Deaux and Tim Emswiller, "Explanations of Successful Performance on Sex-Linked Tasks: What is Skill for the Male is Luck for the Female," *Journal of Personality and Social Psychology,* 1974, *29,* 80-85.
11. Shirley Feldman-Summers and Sara B. Kiesler, "Those Who Are Number Two Try Harder: The Effect of Sex on Attributions of Causality," *Journal of Personality and Social Psychology,* 1974, *30,* 846-855.
12. N. T. Feather and J. G. Simon, "Reactions to Male and Female Success and Failure in Sex-Linked Occupations: Impressions of Personality, Causal Attributions, and Perceived Likelihood of Different Consequences," *Journal of Personality and Social Psychology,* 1975, *31,* 20-31.
13. Kay Deaux and Janet Taynor, "Evaluation of Male and Female Ability: Bias Works Two Ways," *Psychological Reports,* 1973, *32,* 261-262.
14. Feather and Simon, op. cit.
15. Janet Taynor and Kay Deaux, "Equity and Perceived Sex Differences: Role Behavior as Defined by the Task, the Mode, and the Actor," *Journal of Personality and Social Psychology,* 1957, *32,* 381-390.

CHAPTER 4

1. For a complete survey of studies pertaining to self-esteem, as well as a number of other comparisons between the sexes, consult Eleanor Emmons Maccoby and Carol Nagy Jacklin, *The Psychology of Sex Differences* (Stanford, Calif.: Stanford University Press, 1974).
2. Diane L. Boss, "Ramifications of Sex-Role Stereotypes for the Self-Concepts of Males and Females" (unpublished paper, Purdue University, 1974). Her development of this concept was based on a distinction made earlier by E. L. Shostrom, *Personal Orientation Inventory* (San Diego: Educational and Industrial Testing Service, 1966).
3. For example, see Marvin Eisen, "Characteristic Self-Esteem, Sex, and Resistance to Temptation," *Journal of Personality and Social Psychology,* 1972, *24,* 68-72.
4. Consistent differences between men and women on measures of "field dependence" have often been cited to support the argument that women are more influenced by the situation. However, as Maccoby and Jacklin (op. cit.) point out, this particular measure is heavily dependent on visual-spatial abilities, in which men are superior. Other tasks that require "decontextualization" (separating an element from its background) do not show these sex differences.
5. N. T. Feather, "Attribution of Responsibility and Valence of Success and Failure in Relation to Initial Confidence and Task Performance," *Journal of Personality and Social Psychology,* 1969, *13,* 129-144. Also Kay Deaux and Elizabeth Farris, "Attributing Causes for One's Own Performance:

The Effects of Sex, Norms, and Outcome" (unpublished paper, Purdue University, 1974).

6. O. G. Brim, Jr., David C. Glass, J. Neulinger, and Ira J. Firestone, *American Beliefs and Attitudes about Intelligence* (New York: Russell Sage, 1969). Also Ian D. McMahon, "Sex Differences in Causal Attributions Following Success and Failure" (paper presented at meetings of Eastern Psychological Association, April 1972).

7. Virginia C. Crandall, "Sex Differences in Expectancy of Intellectual and Academic Reinforcement," in C. P. Smith (ed.), *Achievement-Related Motives in Children* (New York: Russell Sage, 1969).

8. Dale Soderman Montanelli and Kennedy T. Hill, "Children's Achievement Expectations and Performance as a Function of Two Consecutive Reinforcement Experiences, Sex of Subject, and Sex of Experimenter," *Journal of Personality and Social Psychology,* 1969, *13,* 115-128.

9. Aletha Huston Stein, Sheila Rimland Pohly, and Edward Mueller, "The Influence of Masculine, Feminine, and Neutral Tasks on Children's Achievement Behavior, Expectancies of Success and Attainment Values," *Child Development,* 1971, *42,* 195-207. Also see Deaux and Farris, op. cit.

10. Crandall, op. cit.

11. Deaux and Farris, op. cit.; Feather, op. cit. Also Daniel Bar-Tal and Irene Frieze, "Achievement Motivation and Gender as Determinants of Attributions for Success and Failure" (unpublished manuscript, University of Pittsburgh, 1973).

12. Bar-Tal and Frieze, op. cit.; Feather, op. cit.; Deaux and Farris, op. cit.

13. Maccoby and Jacklin, op. cit.

14. Kay Deaux, Leonard White, and Elizabeth Farris, "Skill versus Luck: Field and Laboratory Studies of Male and Female Preferences," *Journal of Personality and Social Psychology,* 1975, in press.

15. Bar-Tal and Frieze, op. cit.

16. Kay Deaux, "Women in Management: Causal Explanations of Performance" (paper presented at meetings of American Psychological Association, September 1974).

CHAPTER 5

1. David C. McClelland, John W. Atkinson, Russell A. Clark, and Edgar G. Lowell, *The Achievement Motive* (New York: Appleton-Century-Crofts, 1953).

2. Joseph Veroff, Sue Wilcox, and John W. Atkinson, "The Achievement Motive in High School and College Age Women," *Journal of Abnormal and Social Psychology,* 1953, *48,* 108-119.

3. See, for example, the following: W. F. Field, "The Effects of Thematic Apperception on Certain Experimentally Aroused Needs" (unpublished doctoral dissertation, University of Maryland, 1951). See also Gerald S. Lesser, Rhoda N. Krawitz, and Rita Packard, "Experimental Arousal of Achievement Motivation in Adolescent Girls," *Journal of Abnormal and Social Psychology,* 1963, *66,* 59-66.

4. John W. Atkinson and N. T. Feather (eds.), *A Theory of Achievement Motivation* (New York: Wiley, 1966).

5. The expectancy-value theory of Atkinson and Feather includes many more complexities than can be included here. Concepts of the probability of success and incentive value are also introduced, which could be the base of predicting differences between men and women, in line with the discussion in Chapter 4 of expectancy differences.

6. For a thorough discussion of the evidence supporting each of these positions, see Aletha Huston Stein and Margaret M. Bailey, "The Socialization of Achievement Orientation in Females," *Psychological Bulletin,* 1973, *80,* 345-366.

7. Maccoby and Jacklin, op. cit.

8. In addition to those references that will be discussed later, see David Tressemer, "Fear of Success: Popular but Unproven," *Psychology Today,* 1974, 7:10, 82-85; and Matina S. Horner, "Femininity and Successful Achievement: A Basic Inconsistency," in J. M. Bardwick et al., *Feminine Personality and Conflict* (Monterey, Calif.: Brooks/Cole, 1970).

9. Horner, in Bardwick et al., op. cit.

10. Thelma G. Alper, "Achievement Motivation in College Women: A Now-You-See-It—Now-You-Don't Phenomenon," *American Psychologist,* 1974, *29,* 194-203.

11. Janet T. Spence, "The TAT and Attitudes toward Achievement in Women: A New Look at the Motive to Avoid Success and a New Method of Measurement," *Journal of Consulting and Clinical Psychology,* 1974, *42,* 427-437.

12. Alper, op. cit.

13. Matina S. Horner, "Toward an Understanding of Achievement-Related Conflicts in Women," *Journal of Social Issues,* 1972, *28,* 157-175.

14. See, for example, the following: Alfred B. Heilbrun, Jr., Carol Kleemeier, and Gary Piccola, "Developmental and Situational Correlates of Achievement Behavior in College Females," *Journal of Personality,* 1974, *42,* 420-436; and Sandra Schwartz Tangri, "Implied Demand Character of the Wife's Future and Role-Innovation: Patterns of Achievement Orientation among Women," *JSAS Catalog of Selected Documents in Psychology,* 1974, *4,* 12.

15. Lynn Monahan, Deanna Kuhn, and Phillip Shaver, "Intrapsychic versus Cultural Explanations of the 'Fear of Success' Motive," *Journal of Personality and Social Psychology,* 1974, *29,* 60-64.

16. N. T. Feather and Alfred C. Raphelson, "Fear of Success in Australian and American Student Groups: Motive or Sex-Role Stereotype?," *Journal of Personality,* 1974, *42,* 190-201.

17. Alper, op. cit.

18. Frances Cherry and Kay Deaux, "Fear of Success versus Fear of Gender-Inconsistent Behavior: A Sex Similarity" (paper presented at meeting of Midwestern Psychological Association, Chicago, 1975).

19. Vivian P. Makosky, "Fear of Success, Sex-Role Orientation of the Task, and Competitive Conditions as Variables Affecting Women's Performance in Achievement-Oriented Situations" (paper presented at meeting of Midwestern Psychological Association, Cleveland, 1972).

20. Not all attempts have been so successful. Stuart Karabenick and Joan M. Marshall found the predicted relationships for women who were low in fear of failure but not for those who scored high on this measure. ("Performance of Females as a Function of Fear of Success, Fear of Failure, Type of Opponent, and Performance-Contingent Feedback,"

Journal of Personality, 1974, *42*, 220-237.) Sherry Morgan and Bernard Mausner could not find a relationship between measured fear of success and behavior, although all of their female high school subjects showed a tendency to avoid competition with a male partner. ("Behavioral and Fantasied Indicators of Avoidance of Success in Men and Women," *Journal of Personality*, 1973, *41*, 457-470.)

21. Jerald M. Jellison, Renee Jackson-White, and Richard A. Bruder, "Fear of Success? A Situational Approach" (paper presented at meeting of Western Psychological Association, San Francisco, 1974).
22. Jerald M. Jellison, personal communication, 1974.
23. Joan E. Fisher, Edgar C. O'Neal, and Peter J. McDonald, "Female Competitiveness as a Function of Prior Performance Outcome, Competitor's Evaluation, and Sex of Competitor" (paper presented at meeting of Midwestern Psychological Association, Chicago, 1974).
24. Curiously, these authors found exactly the opposite results when the partner of the subject was another female.

CHAPTER 6

1. Eleanor Emmons Maccoby and Carol Nagy Jacklin, *The Psychology of Sex Differences* (Stanford, Calif.: Stanford University Press, 1974).
2. Cheris Kramer, "Women's Speech: Separate but Unequal?," *Quarterly Journal of Speech*, February 1974, 14-24.
3. Cheris Kramer, personal communication, January 1975.
4. Barrie Thorne and Nancy Henley, "Sex Differences in Language, Speech, and Nonverbal Communication" (unpublished manuscript, November 1973).
5. Robin Lakoff, "Language and Woman's Place," *Language in Society*, 1973, *2*, 45-79.
6. Cheris Kramer, "Folk-Linguistics: Wishy-Washy Mommy Talk," *Psychology Today*, June 1974, 82-89.
7. M. H. Landis and H. E. Burtt, "A Study of Conversations," *Journal of Comparative Psychology*, 1924, *4*, 81-89.
8. William F. Soskin and Vera P. John, "The Study of Spontaneous Talk," in Roger Barker (ed.), *The Stream of Behavior* (New York: Appleton-Century-Crofts, 1963).
9. Fred L. Strodtbeck and Richard D. Mann, "Sex Role Differentiation in Jury Deliberations," *Sociometry*, 1956, *19*, 3-11; also Fred L. Strodtbeck, Rita M. James, and Charles Hawkins, "Social Status in Jury Deliberations," *American Sociological Review*, 1957, *22*, 713-719.
10. Don H. Zimmerman and Candy West, "Conversational Order and Sexism: A Convergence of Theoretical and Substantive Problems" (paper presented at Linguistics Conference, California Polytechnic Institute, March 1973). An abstract of this paper is included in the Thorne and Henley bibliography.
11. Landis and Burtt, op. cit. Also H. T. Moore, "Further Data Concerning Sex Differences," *Journal of Abnormal and Social Psychology*, 1922, *4*, 81-89.

12. Elinor Langer, "The Women of the Telephone Company," *New York Review of Books,* March 12 and March 26, 1970.
13. Sidney M. Jourard and P. Lasakow, "Some Factors in Self-Disclosure," *Journal of Abnormal and Social Psychology,* 1958, *56,* 91-98; Sidney M. Jourard, *The Transparent Self* (Princeton, N.J.: Van Nostrand, 1964).
14. Paul C. Cozby, "Self-Disclosure: A Literature Review," *Psychological Bulletin,* 1973, *79,* 73-91.
15. Vello Sermat and Michael Smyth, "Content Analysis of Verbal Communication in the Development of a Relationship: Conditions Influencing Self-Disclosure," *Journal of Personality and Social Psychology,* 1973, *26,* 332-346.
16. Marc Feigen Fasteau, *The Male Machine* (New York: McGraw-Hill, 1974).
17. Sidney M. Jourard, *The Transparent Self.*
18. One exception is a study by Levinger and Senn ("Disclosure Feelings in Marriage," *Merrill-Palmer Quarterly,* 1967, *13,* 237-249). Husbands and wives were asked what proportion of their pleasant and unpleasant feelings they disclosed to their spouses, and no differences were found. Husbands did perceive that their wives disclosed relatively more unpleasant feelings. However, because this study only asked for self-reports, we can't be sure what the actual levels of self-disclosure were.
19. Ralph V. Exline, "Explorations in the Process of Person Perception: Visual Interaction in Relation to Competition, Sex, and Need for Affiliation," *Journal of Personality,* 1963, *31,* 1-20; Ralph Exline, David Gray, and Dorothy Shuette, "Visual Behavior in a Dyad as Affected by Interview Content and Sex of Respondent," *Journal of Personality and Social Psychology,* 1965, *1,* 201-209.
20. Michael Argyle, Mansur Lalljee, and Mark Cook, "The Effects of Visibility on Interaction in a Dyad," *Human Relations,* 1968, *21,* 3-17.
21. Ross W. Buck, Virginia J. Savin, Robert E. Miller, and William F. Caul, "Communication of Affect through Facial Expressions in Humans," *Journal of Personality and Social Psychology,* 1972, *23,* 362-371.
22. Ross Buck, Robert E. Miller, and William F. Caul, "Sex, Personality, and Physiological Variables in the Communication of Affect via Facial Expression," *Journal of Personality and Social Psychology,* 1974, *30,* 587-596.
23. Allen I. Schiffenbauer and Amy Babineau, "The Effects of Sex of Stimulus, Sex of Judge, and Intensity of Expression, on the Spontaneous Attribution of Emotion," *Journal of Research in Personality,* in press.
24. Jane van Lawick-Goodall, *In the Shadow of Man* (Boston: Houghton Mifflin, 1971).
25. Daphne E. Bugental, Leonore R. Love, and Robert M. Gianetto, "Perfidious Feminine Faces," *Journal of Personality and Social Psychology,* 1971, *17,* 314-318. Also Daphne E. Bugental, Jaques W. Kaswan, and Leonore R. Love, "Perception of Contradictory Meanings Conveyed by Verbal and Nonverbal Channels," *Journal of Personality and Social Psychology,* 1970, *16,* 647-655.
26. Robert Rosenthal, Dane Archer, M. Robin DiMatteo, Judith Hall Koivumaki, and Peter L. Rogers, "Body Talk and Tone of Voice: The Language without Words," *Psychology Today,* September 1974, 64-68.
27. Nancy M. Henley, "The Politics of Touch," in Phil Brown (ed.), *Radical Psychology* (New York: Harper & Row, 1973), pp. 421-433. Also Nancy M. Henley, "Status and Sex: Some Touching Observations," *Bulletin of the Psychonomic Society,* 1973, *2,* 91-93.

28. Jeffrey D. Fisher, Marvin Rytting, and Richard Heslin, "Hands Touching Hands: Affective and Evaluative Effects of an Interpersonal Touch" (paper presented at meeting of Midwestern Psychological Association, Chicago, May 1975).
29. Henley, op. cit.
30. James C. Baxer, "Interpersonal Spacing in Natural Settings," *Sociometry,* 1970, *33,* 444-456.
31. Jeffrey David Fisher, "Attitude Similarity as a Determinant of Perceived Crowdedness and Perceived Environmental Quality: Support for an Interactive Model for Prediction of the Behavioral Effects of Density and Other Environmental Stimuli" (unpublished master's thesis, Purdue University, 1973).
32. Michael Argyle and Janet Dean, "Eye Contact, Distance and Affiliation," *Sociometry,* 1965, *28,* 289-304.
33. M. Horowitz, D. Duff, and L. Stratton, "Body-Buffer Zone," *Archives of General Psychiatry,* 1964, *146,* 24-35.
34. Jeffrey David Fisher and Donn Byrne, "Too Close for Comfort: Sex Differences in Response to Invasions of Personal Space," *Journal of Personality and Social Psychology,* 1975, *32,* 15-21.
35. Maccoby and Jacklin, op. cit.

CHAPTER 7

1. Actually, the origin of this particular custom is a topic of dispute. Some historians claim that the splash from carriages on the street was the basis of the custom, while others cling to the garbage theory. In either case, the result was men walking on the "curb" side of the walk.
2. Bibb Latané and James M. Dabbs, Jr., "Sex and Helping in Columbus, Seattle, and Atlanta" (paper presented at meeting of American Psychological Association, Honolulu, August 1972).
3. Irving M. Piliavin, Judith Rodin, and Jane A. Piliavin, "Good Samaritanism: An Underground Phenomenon?," *Journal of Personality and Social Psychology,* 1969, *13,* 289-299.
4. James H. Bryan and Mary Ann Test, "Models and Helping: Naturalistic Studies in Aiding Behavior," *Journal of Personality and Social Psychology,* 1967, *6,* 400-407.
5. Robert Athanasiou and Paul Greene, "Physical Attractiveness and Helping Behavior" (paper presented at meetings of American Psychological Association, Montreal, August 1973).
6. Richard J. Pomazal and Gerald L. Clore, "Helping on the Highway: The Effects of Dependency and Sex," *Journal of Applied Social Psychology,* 1973, *3,* 150-164.
7. Martin K. Moss and Richard A. Page, "Reinforcement and Helping Behavior," *Journal of Applied Social Psychology,* 1972, *2,* 360-371.
8. Alan E. Gross, "Sex and Helping: Intrinsic Glow and Extrinsic Show" (paper presented at meeting of American Psychological Association, Honolulu, September 1972). The results of this study are somewhat more complicated. Though men and women showed an equal tendency to help when they were in the company of another person, the helping behavior of men dropped sharply when they were alone. Women continued to show

the same amount of help when no one was present to witness the act. One possible explanation for these findings is that men are more dependent on social reinforcement, while women have a stronger intrinsic motivation for helping others. More studies of this totally anonymous form of help will have to be conducted before we can make any conclusions about these differences.

9. Charles L. Gruder and Thomas D. Cook, "Sex, Dependency, and Helping," *Journal of Personality and Social Psychology*, 1971, *19*, 290-294.
10. Samuel Gaertner and Leonard Bickman, "Effects of Race on the Elicitation of Helping Behavior: The Wrong Number Technique," *Journal of Personality and Social Psychology*, 1971, *20*, 218-222.
11. Cheryl Primmer, James Jaccard, Jerry L. Cohen, Julie Wasserman, and Ann Hoffing, "The Influence of the Sex-Appropriateness of a Task on Helping Behavior in the Laboratory and the Field" (unpublished manuscript, University of Illinois, 1974).
12. Leonard Bickman, "Sex and Helping Behavior," *Journal of Social Psychology*, 1974, *93*, 43-53.
13. Frances Cherry, "Sex Differences in Attraction as a Function of Interpersonal Feedback" (unpublished manuscript, Indiana University, 1974).
14. Bibb Latané and John Darley, *The Unresponsive Bystander: Why Doesn't He Help?* (New York: Appleton-Century-Crofts, 1970).
15. Stephen Thayer, "Lend Me Your Ears: Racial and Sexual Factors in Helping the Deaf," *Journal of Personality and Social Psychology*, 1973, *28*, 8-11.
16. Tim Emswiller, Kay Deaux, and Jerry E. Willits, "Similarity, Sex, and Requests for Small Favors," *Journal of Applied Social Psychology*, 1971, *1*, 284-291.
17. In one study (Mary B. Harris and Gail Bays, "Altruism and Sex Roles," *Psychological Reports*, 1973, *32*, 1002), the attractiveness of a woman asking for help was varied, and it was found that more attractive women received more help from men. For women helpers, the attractiveness of the female requester was not a significant factor. Because this study did not include male requesters of varying attractiveness, we cannot make strong conclusions about the importance of liking in cross-sex interactions. The results are consistent, however, with the general argument presented.
18. Michael Hendricks, Thomas D. Cook, and William D. Crano, "Sex and a Prior Favor as Moderators of Helping" (paper presented at meeting of Midwestern Psychological Association, Chicago, May 1973).

CHAPTER 8

1. Fran Cherry and I have analyzed a number of the traditional areas of social-psychological research in terms of this subject selection. Other areas that reflect a similar male bias include achievement, leadership, and the risky shift.
2. Albert Bandura, "Influence of Models' Reinforcement Contingencies on the Acquisition of Imitative Responses," *Journal of Personality and Social Psychology*, 1965, *1*, 589-595.

3. Arnold H. Buss, "Physical Aggression in Relation to Different Frustrations," *Journal of Abnormal and Social Psychology*, 1963, *67*, 1-7.
4. Wesley Kilham and Leon Mann, "Level of Destructive Obedience as a Function of Transmitter and Executant Roles in the Milgram Obedience Paradigm," *Journal of Personality and Social Psychology*, 1974, *29*, 696-702.
5. When people are simply given a written description of this situation and asked to predict what others would do, their predictions show the same pattern, reflecting a belief that men would give more shock than would women (Arthur G. Miller and Shirley Radlove, "The Prediction and Perception of Obedience to Authority," *Journal of Personality*, 1974, *42*, 23-42). Adherents to the belief of greater female compliance may find these results surprising, but as we shall see in Chapter 9, compliance is probably a multidetermined behavior.
6. Stuart P. Taylor and Seymour Epstein, "Aggression as a Function of the Interaction of the Sex of the Aggressor and the Sex of the Victim," *Journal of Personality*, 1967, *35*, 473-486.
7. Jack E. Hokanson and Robert Edelman, "Effects of Three Social Responses on Vascular Processes," *Journal of Personality and Social Psychology*, 1966, *3*, 442-447.
8. Jack E. Hokanson, K. R. Willers, and Elizabeth Koropsak, "The Modification of Autonomic Responses during Aggressive Interchange," *Journal of Personality*, 1968, *36*, 386-404.
9. In a recent report, Marla Martinolich and Lee Sechrest have suggested the findings of studies using electric shock may not be replicated when a different form of aggression, such as a noxious noise, is used. They report that few sex differences are found in this latter case. ("Physical Aggression as a Function of Sex of Subject, Sex of Target, and Subject's Attitude toward the Role of Women," paper presented at meeting of Southeastern Psychological Association, Atlanta, March 1975.) Future research should consider the possibility of such differences.
10. Anthony N. Doob and Alan E. Gross, "Status of Frustrator as an Inhibitor of Horn-Honking Responses," *Journal of Social Psychology*, 1968, *76*, 213-218.
11. Kay K. Deaux, "Honking at the Intersection: A Replication and Extension," *Journal of Social Psychology*, 1971, *84*, 159-160.
12. Mary B. Harris, "Mediators between Frustration and Aggression in a Field Experiment," *Journal of Experimental Social Psychology*, 1974, *10*, 561-571.
13. Mary B. Harris, "Field Studies of Modeled Aggression," *Journal of Social Psychology*, 1973, *89*, 131-139.
14. In some of the Buss experiments, the subject is insulted by the confederate prior to the learning phase, which would give some basis for arguing that the teacher was simply reacting to an initially aggressive behavior by the learner. However, giving a painful shock is clearly upping the ante, and it still seems reasonable to consider this a case of instigation.
15. Sociologist Murray Straus has written a number of articles on aggression and violence in the family setting. See, for example, the following: Murray A. Straus, "A General Systems Theory Approach to a Theory of Violence between Family Members," *Social Science Information*, 1973, *12*, 105-125; also Suzanne K. Steinmetz and Murray A. Straus, "The Family as Cradle of Violence," *Society* (formerly *Transaction*), 1974, *10*, 50-56.

16. Buss, op. cit.
17. Taylor and Epstein, op. cit.
18. Harris, *Journal of Social Psychology,* op. cit.
19. Deaux, op. cit.
20. Robert J. Kaleta and Arnold H. Buss, "Aggression Intensity and Femininity of the Victim" (paper presented at meeting of Eastern Psychological Association, May 1973).
21. David M. Young, Ernst G. Beier, Paul Beier, and Cole Barton, "Aggression as Communication: A Study in Chivalry," *Journal of Communication,* 1975, in press.
22. A discussion of this issue has been presented by *Ms. Magazine* (Letty Cottin Pogrebin, "Do Women Make Men Violent?," November 1974, pp. 49-55, 80).
23. Richard J. Borden, "Influence of an Observer's Sex and Values on Aggressive Responding," *Journal of Personality and Social Psychology,* 1975, *31,* 567-573.

CHAPTER 9

1. Irving L. Janis and P. B. Field, "Sex Differences and Personality Factors Related to Persuasibility," in I. L. Janis et al. (eds.), *Personality and Persuasibility* (New Haven: Yale University Press, 1959).
2. Solomon E. Asch, "Studies of Independence and Conformity: A Minority of One against a Unanimous Majority," *Psychological Monographs,* 1956, *70* (9, Whole No. 416).
3. For a summary of these studies, see Eleanor Emmons Maccoby and Carol Nagy Jacklin, *The Psychology of Sex Differences* (Stanford, Calif.: Stanford University Press, 1974).
4. Frank Sistrunk and John W. McDavid, "Sex Variable in Conforming Behavior," *Journal of Personality and Social Psychology,* 1971, *17,* 200-207.
5. Anatol Rapoport and Albert M. Chammah, "Sex Differences in Factors Contributing to the Level of Cooperation in the Prisoner's Game." *Journal of Personality and Social Psychology,* 1965, *2,* 831-838; also Jeffrey Bedell and Frank Sistrunk, "Power, Opportunity Costs, and Sex in a Mixed-Motive Game," *Journal of Personality and Social Psychology,* 1973, *25,* 219-226.
6. Charlan Nemeth, "A Critical Analysis of Research Utilizing the Prisoner's Dilemma Paradigm for the Study of Bargaining," in L. Berkowitz (ed.), *Advances in Experimental Social Psychology,* vol. 6 (New York: Academic Press, 1973).
7. Robert S. Wyer, Jr., and Christine Malinowski, "Effects of Sex and Achievement Level upon Individualism and Competitiveness in Social Interaction," *Journal of Experimental Social Psychology,* 1972, *8,* 303-314.
8. Arnold Kahn, Joe Hottes, and William L. Davis, "Cooperation and Optimal Responding in the Prisoner's Dilemma Game: Effects of Sex and Physical Attractiveness," *Journal of Personality and Social Psychology,* 1971, *17,* 267-279.

9.   Joseph H. Hottes and Arnold Kahn, "Sex Differences in a Mixed-Motive Conflict Situation," *Journal of Personality*, 1974, *42*, 260-275.
10. Terry E. Black and Kenneth L. Higbee, "Effects of Power, Threat, and Sex on Exploitation," *Journal of Personality and Social Psychology*, 1973, *27*, 382-388.
11. W. Edgar Vinacke, "Sex-Roles in a Three-Person Game," *Sociometry*, 1959, *22*, 343-360; also John R. Bond and W. Edgar Vinacke, "Coalitions in Mixed-Sex Triads," *Sociometry*, 1961, *24*, 61-75.
12. Alan W. Wicker and Gary Bushweiler, "Perceived Fairness and Pleasantness of Social Exchange Situations: Two Factorial Studies of Inequity," *Journal of Personality and Social Psychology*, 1970, *15*, 63-75.
13. Gerald S. Leventhal and Douglas W. Lane, "Sex, Age and Equity Behavior," *Journal of Personality and Social Psychology*, 1970, *15*, 312-316.
14. Gerald S. Leventhal and David Anderson, "Self-Interest and Maintenance of Equity," *Journal of Personality and Social Psychology*, 1970, *15*, 57-62; also I. M. Lane and Lawrence Messé, "Equity and Distribution of Rewards," *Journal of Personality and Social Psychology*, 1971, *20*, 1-17.
15. Lawrence A. Messé and Charlene M. Callahan, "Sex and Message Effects in Reward Allocation Behavior" (unpublished manuscript, Michigan State University, 1974).
16. Gerald S. Leventhal, "Reward Allocation by Males and Females" (paper presented at meeting of American Psychological Association, Montreal, September 1973).
17. Leventhal and Lane, op. cit. Although Messé and Callahan ("Sex Differences in the Allocation of Pay," unpublished manuscript, Michigan State University, 1974) did not find significant differences in the self-evaluation of males and females, their scale was quite restricted and may have precluded the detection of subtle differences.
18. Martha Shuch Mednick and Sandra Schwartz Tangri, "New Social Psychological Perspectives on Women," *Journal of Social Issues*, 1972, *28*, 1-16.
19. Arnold Kahn, "Reactions to Generosity or Stinginess from an Intelligent or Stupid Work Partner: A Test of Equity Theory in a Direct Exchange Relationship," *Journal of Personality and Social Psychology*, 1972, *21*, 117-123.
20. Jacquelyn W. Gaebelein, "Instigative Aggression in Females," *Psychological Reports*, 1973, *33*, 619-622.
21. Howard Garland and Burt R. Brown, "Face-Saving as Affected by Subjects' Sex, Audiences' Sex, and Audience Expertise," *Sociometry*, 1972, *35*, 280-289.
22. Kahn, op. cit.
23. Jacquelyn Gaebelein (op. cit.) has found that the performance of women is related to cooperation in the same situation in which men respond to financial incentives.

CHAPTER 10

1.   Lionel Tiger, *Men in Groups* (New York: Random House, 1969).

2. Roland Radloff and Robert Helmreich, *Groups under Stress: Psychological Research in Sealab II* (New York: Appleton-Century-Crofts, 1968).
3. Alan Booth, "Sex and Social Participation," *American Sociological Review,* 1972, *37,* 183-193.
4. Marc Feigen Fasteau, *The Male Machine* (New York: McGraw-Hill, 1974).
5. Fred L. Strodtbeck and Richard O. Mann, "Sex Role Differences in Jury Deliberations," *Sociometry,* 1956, *19,* 3-11.
6. Jane Allyn Piliavin and Rachel Rosemann Martin, "The Effects of the Sex Composition of Groups on Style of Social Interaction" (unpublished manuscript, University of Wisconsin, 1974).
7. It is interesting to consider how these stylistic differences between women and men might be seen in more natural group settings. Consciousness-raising groups are an intriguing example. While no systematic research has been done with these groups, there are many informal reports of their activities. (See Joseph H. Pleck and Jack Sawyer (eds.), *Men and Masculinity,* Englewood Cliffs, N.J.: Prentice-Hall, 1974; also Letty Cottin Pogrebin, "Rap Groups: The Feminist Connection," *Ms.,* March 1973, p. 80 ff.) A reading of these reports suggests the possibility that the men's groups indeed find expressive behavior more difficult than do women's groups. Developing instrumental behaviors, in contrast, seems to crop up more frequently in reports of women's groups.
8. Jonathan L. Freedman, Alan S. Levy, Roberta Welte Buchanan, and Judy Price, "Crowding and Human Aggressiveness," *Journal of Experimental Social Psychology,* 1972, *8,* 528-548.
9. Michael Ross, Bruce Layton, Bonnie Ericson, and John Schopler, "Affect, Facial Regard, and Reactions to Crowding," *Journal of Personality and Social Psychology,* 1973, *28,* 69-76.
10. Andrew P. Schettino and Richard J. Borden, "Group Size versus Group Density: Where Is the Affect?" (unpublished paper, Purdue University, 1975).
11. Joan E. Marshall and Richard Heslin, "Boys and Girls Together: Sexual Composition and the Effect of Density and Group Size on Cohesiveness," *Journal of Personality and Social Psychology,* 1975, *31,* 952-961.
12. *That 51 Per Cent: Ford Foundation Activities Related to Opportunities for Women* (New York: The Ford Foundation, 1974), p. 15.
13. Edwin Megargee, "Influence of Sex Roles on the Manifestation of Leadership," *Journal of Applied Psychology,* 1969, *53,* 377-382.
14. A comprehensive summary of this material can be found in Virginia E. O'Leary, "Some Attitudinal Barriers to Occupational Aspirations in Women," *Psychological Bulletin,* 1974, *81,* 809-826.
15. Marsha B. Jacobson and Joan Effertz, "Sex Roles and Leadership: Perceptions of the Leaders and the Led," *Organizational Behavior and Human Performance,* 1974, *12,* 383-396.

CHAPTER 11

1. For a fascinating and more detailed discussion of interpersonal attraction, see Zick Rubin, *Liking and Loving: An Invitation to Social Psychology* (New York: Holt, Rinehart & Winston, 1973).
2. Reported in the Wall Street Journal, February 26, 1974.

3. Robert H. Coombs and William F. Kenkel, "Sex Differences in Dating Aspirations and Satisfaction with Computer-Selected Partners," *Journal of Marriage and the Family*, 1966, *28*, 62-66.
4. Ellen Berscheid and Elaine Walster, "Physical Attractiveness," in L. Berkowitz (ed.), *Advances in Experimental Social Psychology*, vol. 7 (New York: Academic Press, 1974). See also Donn Byrne, Charles R. Ervin, and John Lamberth, "Continuity between the Experimental Study of Attraction and Real-Life Computer Dating," *Journal of Personality and Social Psychology*, 1970, *16*, 157-165; and James P. Curran, "Correlates of Physical Attractiveness and Interpersonal Attraction in the Dating Situation," *Social Behavior and Personality*, 1973, *1*, 153-157.
5. James P. Curran, "Differential Effects of Stated Preferences and Questionnaire Role Performance on Interpersonal Attraction in the Dating Situation," *Journal of Psychology*, 1972, *82*, 313-327.
6. Berscheid and Walster, op. cit.
7. For lengthier presentation of these theories, see Donn Byrne, *The Attraction Paradigm* (New York: Academic Press, 1971); and Z. Rubin, op. cit.
8. Byrne, Ervin, and Lamberth, op. cit. Also, Donn Byrne, Oliver London, and Keith Reeves, "The Effects of Physical Attractiveness, Sex, and Attitude Similarity on Interpersonal Attraction," *Journal of Personality*, 1968, *36*, 259-271.
9. John C. Touhey, "Comparison of Two Dimensions of Attitude Similarity on Heterosexual Attraction," *Journal of Personality and Social Psychology*, 1972, *23*, 8-10.
10. Mark S. Cary, "Nonverbal Openings to Conversations" (paper presented at meeting of Eastern Psychological Association, Philadelphia, April 1974).
11. Chris L. Kleinke, Richard A. Staneski, and Pam Weaver, "Evaluation of a Person Who Uses Another's Name in Ingratiating and Noningratiating Situations," *Journal of Experimental Social Psychology*, 1972, *8*, 457-466.
12. Chris L. Kleinke, Armando A. Bustos, Frederick B. Meeker, and Richard A. Staneski, "Effects of Self-Attributed and Other-Attributed Gaze on Interpersonal Evaluations between Males and Females," *Journal of Experimental Social Psychology*, 1973, *9*, 154-163.
13. Coombs and Kenkel, op. cit.
14. Rubin, op. cit.
15. Alan C. Kerckhoff and Keith E. Davis, "Value Consensus and Need Complementarity in Mate Selection," *American Sociological Review*, 1962, *27*, 295-303.
16. Robert F. Winch, *Mate-Selection: A Study of Complementary Needs* (New York: Harper & Row, 1958).
17. Kerckhoff and Davis, op. cit.; Winch, op. cit.
18. George Levinger, David J. Senn, and Bruce W. Jorgensen, "Progress toward Permanence in Courtship: A Test of the Kerckhoff-Davis Hypothesis," *Sociometry*, 1970, *33*, 427-443.
19. Talcott Parsons and Robert F. Bales, *Family, Socialization, and Interaction Process* (New York: Free Press, 1960).
20. For examples of these nonconforming studies, see the following: R. K. Leik, "Instrumentality and Emotionality in Family Interaction," *Sociometry*, 1963, *26*, 131-145; J. F. O'Rourke, "Field and Laboratory: The Decision-Making Behavior of Family Groups in Two Experimental Conditions," *Sociometry*, 1963, *26*, 422-435.

CHAPTER 12

1. Anne Constantinople, "Masculinity-Femininity: An Exception to a Fa-
    mous Dictum?," *Psychological Bulletin,* 1973, *80,* 389-407. (This article
    provides an extensive discussion of the validity of various M-F scales.)
2. Constantinople, op. cit.
3. D. R. Disher, "Regional Differences in Masculinity-Femininity Re-
    sponses," *Journal of Social Psychology,* 1942, *15,* 53-61.
4. Ravenna Helson, "Personality of Women with Imaginative and Artistic
    Interests: The Role of Masculinity, Originality, and Other Characteristics
    in their Creativity," *Journal of Personality,* 1966, *34,* 1-25.
5. Joseph F. Rychlak, Donald L. Tasto, Joanne E. Andrews, and H. Case
    Ellis, "The Application of an Affective Dimension of Meaningfulness to
    Personality-Related Verbal Learning," *Journal of Personality,* 1973, *41,*
    341-360.
6. Carolyn G. Heilbrun, *Toward a Recognition of Androgyny* (New York:
    Knopf, 1973).
7. Sandra L. Bem, "The Measurement of Psychological Androgyny," *Journal
    of Consulting and Clinical Psychology,* 1974, *42,* 155-162.
8. A similar conception of the benefits of androgyny has been presented by
    Jeanne H. Block ("Conceptions of Sex Role: Some Cross-Cultural and
    Longitudinal Perspectives," *American Psychologist,* 1973, *28,* 512-526).
9. Bem, op. cit.
10. Janet T. Spence, Robert Helmreich, and Joy Stapp, "Ratings of Self and
    Peers on Sex-Role Attributes and Their Relation to Self-Esteem and
    Conceptions of Masculinity and Femininity," *Journal of Personality and
    Social Psychology,* in press; also Janet T. Spence, personal communication,
    1975.
11. In fairness to these investigators, it should be acknowledged that they are
    less interested in the concept of androgyny *per se* and more interested in
    the dualism of masculinity and femininity. They would argue that on some
    occasions a single dimension may be most predictive, while a combination
    of the two would be a better predictor on other occasions.
12. Eleanor E. Maccoby, "Sex Differences in Intellectual Functioning," in E.
    E. Maccoby (ed.), *The Development of Sex Differences* (Stanford, Calif.:
    Stanford University Press, 1966).
13. Sandra L. Bem, "Psychology Looks at Sex Roles: Where Have All the
    Androgynous People Gone?" (paper presented at UCLA Symposium on
    Women, May 1972).
14. Spence, Helmreich, and Stapp, op. cit.
15. A more basic and fascinating question concerns the origin of androgyny.
    Why do some boys and girls become androgynous, while others develop
    more traditionally sex-typed traits? Janet Spence and her colleagues are
    beginning to investigate the connections between the masculinity and
    femininity of parents and their children, but the results are unfortunately
    still in a very preliminary stage.
16. Sandra L. Bem, "Sex-Role Adaptability: One Consequence of Psycho-
    logical Androgyny," *Journal of Personality and Social Psychology,* 1975,
    31, 634-643.
17. Sandra L. Bem and Ellen Lenney, "Sex-Typing and the Avoidance of
    Cross-Sex Behavior," *Journal of Personality and Social Psychology,* in
    press.

Name Index

Subject Index